Executive Summary

Background

The U.S. Department of Justice Office of Community Oriented Policing Services (COPS) was directed by the Consolidated Appropriations Act, 2004, to submit a report to Congress on "best practices" developed by law enforcement to secure special events of national or regional importance, such as sporting events, concerts, and cultural exhibitions. The report, "Planning and Managing Security for Major Special Events: Guidelines for Law Enforcement," was prepared after a nationwide study that included:

- Consultations with representatives of the Department of Homeland Security (DHS), U.S. Secret Service, Federal Bureau of Investigation (FBI), and other agencies charged with providing high levels of security for major national events.

- Interviews with private security experts regarding such events as National Football League and National Basketball Association games.

- On-site observations of security planning and management for the Republican and Democratic National Conventions, Kentucky Derby, and other major events.

- Extensive telephone interviews with more than 40 local law enforcement agencies concerning best practices for securing major events in their jurisdictions.

- Reviews of relevant security plans, reports, articles, guidelines, and other documents produced by experts in event security planning and management.

Purpose of the Guidelines Report

The guidelines report provides a framework to assist local law enforcement in planning and managing security for events that attract large numbers of people. It includes examples of best practices employed by federal agencies with security responsibilities, as well as strategies that have been effective for local law enforcement and private security. The focus is on national and regional events, which often include a variety of VIPs and may be targets for terrorists, other criminals, and protestors. The variety of approaches discussed can be tailored to large or small local special events.

Challenges and Principles

In planning and managing major special events, law enforcement must:

- Plan for worst-case scenarios—extraordinary crimes, violence by protestors, a possible terrorist attack, natural disasters—but also be thoroughly prepared to deal with ordinary crimes and incidents (fights, drunkenness, etc.).

- Weigh the security measures that conceivably could be taken (e.g., street closures, searches, highly visible tactical units) against the jurisdiction's desire to produce events that are enjoyable, well attended, and profitable.

- Ensure that the event continues safely and at the same time respect Constitutional rights, including freedom of speech and assembly.

- Establish new and effective—but temporary—organizational arrangements, management structures, and methods of communication.

- Ensure that the rest of the jurisdiction receives essential law enforcement services, regardless of the size or importance of the event.

- Ensure that appropriate federal officials, such as DHS State Homeland Security Advisors, are informed in advance about events with national or international significance to guarantee federal awareness and possible support.

The guidelines report offers principles for major event planning and management that recognize these challenges. The most obvious principle—one that many in law enforcement said cannot be overstated—is that timely, effective planning, communication, and training are critical.

Pre-Event Planning

Pre-event planning should begin 12-18 months before the date of the event, if possible. At the federal level, pre-event planning may begin two to three years prior to a major special event. Often, major national and regional events involve multiple federal, state, and local law enforcement agencies. Additional key partners include fire, emergency medical services (EMS), transportation, public works, health, and other public agencies and the private sector—businesses affected by the event, as well as private security.

Leadership Authority and Structure

Governing bodies must define events that require the highest levels of law enforcement attention to security. For example, the Secretary of DHS, after consultation with the Homeland Security Counsel, is responsible for designating National Special Security Events (NSSEs). NSSEs are significant domestic or international events, which, by virtue of their profile or status, represent a significant target, and warrant additional preparation, planning and mitigation efforts. By definition, an NSSE is an Incident of National Significance as defined by the National Response Plan.

By Presidential directive, the U.S. Secret Service is the lead agency for the design and implementation of the operational security plan for the NSSE. The FBI is the lead federal agency for crisis management, counterterrorism, hostage rescue, and intelligence, and the Federal Emergency Management Agency (FEMA) is the lead federal agency for consequence management (response and recovery operations).

Many special events are held on private property, with leadership shared among the venue owner/private security and the local police and fire departments. Even when one law enforcement agency clearly has the lead and provides most of the resources—a July 4th celebration in a city park, for example—assistance from other law enforcement agencies may be needed (e.g., sheriff's office for prisoner transport, county police for standby tactical support).

Inter-agency Agreement. In multiple agency situations, a simple, straightforward memorandum of understanding (MOU) or agreement (MOA) should be signed. It is critical to clarify the legal authority of assisting agencies to enforce the law in the lead agency's jurisdiction. This may not be covered by existing mutual aid agreements. For example, the Boston Police Department needed to involve many other law enforcement agencies to assist with the 2004 Democratic National Convention, but its existing mutual aid pacts covered only "emergencies" strictly defined as natural disasters. It needed help from the county sheriff to deputize outside law enforcement officers, military personnel, National Guard members, and others. The MOU or MOA should also enumerate the commitment of assisting agencies in providing personnel and equipment; state when and where other agencies' officers should arrive and the specifics of their assignments (duty posts, shifts, etc.); and clarify any compensation for labor costs, expenses, and equipment incurred by the assisting agencies.

Executive Team and Subcommittee Model. Most major event planning begins with creation of an executive team headed by the overall event security director who represents the lead law enforcement agency. This team typically involves top command level personnel from all partners in securing the event.

Key tasks:

- Identify all functional areas that need to be planned, create subcommittees to handle those areas, and issue timelines—who will plan what by when.

- Review subcommittee operational plans to ensure that they are comprehensive, consistent, and realistic, and that contingency plans are in place for each major function.

- Determine any changes needed in routine policies, practices, or laws (e.g., does the union contract permit 12-hour shifts to cover a major special event?).

Subcommittees vary depending on the event, but 20 or more responsibility areas may be identified, including personnel resources; legal issues; communications; intelligence; field operations/venue safety and security; transportation/traffic; tactical support; fire/EMS/hospital services; prisoner processing; credentialing; media relations; training; budget and logistics; and after-action evaluation. Additional areas (especially for NSSEs) include airspace security; critical infrastructure/utilities; hazardous materials/weapons of mass destruction; consequence management; crisis management; and cyber-security.

Threat and Risk Assessments

The FBI, DHS, and International Association of Assembly Managers are among the organizations that offer criteria for classifying special events according to threat levels and corresponding security levels. The FBI uses eight factors to arrive at four Special Event Readiness Levels (SERLs). The SERLs relate to anticipated levels of FBI support, but the eight factors are relevant to local law enforcement: size of event; threat (including known threats to the specific event); historical, political, or symbolic significance; duration; location; cultural, political, and religious backgrounds of attendees; media coverage; and dignitaries attending.

Key Assessment Areas. Comprehensive threat and risk assessments involve (1) identifying potential threats, including common crimes (robbery, assault, etc.), fires, vandalism, natural disasters, protests, terrorism, or gangs; (2) gauging potential damages from such threats (impact analysis); (3) determining the likelihood that the problems will occur; and (4) developing cost estimates and actions to prevent the threats.

Resources. Guidelines and formulas for conducting threat and risk assessments are available from DHS and take into account the intention and capability of an adversary, as well as vulnerabilities (e.g., building characteristics, security practices). The U.S. Secret Service has also developed threat assessment tools, primarily regarding protection of targets.

Threat and Risk Categories. The main threat and risk categories are (1) harm to persons; (2) damage to property; (3) loss of revenue for the event and jurisdiction if incidents prevent people from attending or cause increased expenses; (4) increased liability due to negligence; and (5) loss of reputation—tourists may not come to the jurisdiction or event again because of problems.

Information Collection. General guidelines for the information collection phase are provided in the full report, with additional details available from other sources. Briefly, critical tasks are to:

- Assign responsibility to experienced, qualified assessors

- Review available information (floor plans, utility layouts, maps, aerial photos, evacuation plans, fire inspection reports, etc.)

- Interview event planners in the governing jurisdiction and the event promoters

- Obtain threat intelligence information from internal and external sources

- Conduct extensive site observations and surveys

- Develop detailed participant profiles

- Assess the security plans of key event hotels

- Examine all forms of transportation that participants will use to travel to the event— airports, trains, buses, subways, etc.

Other Threats and Impacts

- Cyber Vulnerability. One of the greatest threats to the security of future special events may be cyber attack. The U.S. Secret Service, in cooperation with Carnegie Mellon University, has been leading the effort to develop cyber vulnerability assessments for major special events.

- Business Impact Analysis. Although special events can mean increased revenues for businesses, the opposite may be the case (e.g., temporary Jersey barriers block access). It is incumbent on law enforcement, in planning for special event security measures, to assess the likely impact on local businesses.

Responsibility Areas

The guidelines report discusses each responsibility area in major special event planning and management. Only a few of the key considerations in each area are represented in this summary.

(1) Determining and Acquiring the Security Workforce

Workforce issues that are part of planning for any major special event include the following:

- What are all of the security assignments/posts that require staffing (inner, middle, and outer perimeter; transit routes; etc.)?

- How many personnel will be needed at each assignment/post?

- How many supervisors will be needed for each assignment/post?

- How long will shifts last (8 hours, 12 hours)?

- How much relief will be needed?

- Will our own officers and officers from outside agencies be paid overtime?

- What different types of skills are needed (information technology, administrative support, dispatchers, canine handlers, bike patrol, mounted, etc.)?

- What different types of authority are needed (e.g., prosecutors, civil attorneys)?

- Will officers need security clearances if they intend to receive federal intelligence information?

Various law enforcement agencies interviewed for this report offered advice related to assigning sufficient personnel to major special events. For example:

- Have a sufficient "show of force" for events with a history of disruptions.

- Have crowd control officers on standby at the site of major national sporting events (e.g., the World Series).

- Don't underestimate the need for relief personnel. Officers, supervisors, and commanders become exhausted without good scheduling and sufficient relief.

- When key contacts are identified in the lead and assisting agencies, also designate back-up personnel. Staff turnover may well occur before the event takes place.

The guidelines report also discusses various specialized services deployed by law enforcement to provide safety and security. These include:

- Explosive detection canines and handlers. These are used extensively for national events and often—although not necessarily as a matter of routine—for major regional and local events. Generally, the perceived value of explosive detection canines depends on the extent to which an area can be secured after a sweep.

- Mounted units. Law enforcement agencies with mounted units consistently praised the advantages of horses as a "force multiplier." The main drawback was cost (some mounted units had been cut back because of overall budget cuts).

- Bicycle units. Key advantages include quick access to various areas and crowd control (when bicycles are lined up as a "portable fence").

- Crisis management units. Assets that can be deployed proactively during major special events to address crisis management issues such as explosives ordinance disposal (EOD), tactical teams, and intelligence teams.

- Other units. Depending on the nature of the event and associated threats, law enforcement may deploy gang, drug, fraud, vice, and other specialists, such as a post-blast investigation team or dive team to supplement water support such as the Coast Guard.

Private Security. The private sector owns the organizations, and often the facilities, involved in many of the major sporting events, concerts, and other public entertainment in the United States. Often, the owners have hired their own private security. Private security may take the lead role in securing the event or take a supporting role to law enforcement. Regardless of the exact nature of the working relationship, private security plays a vital role, and law enforcement must be prepared to partner with private security.

Hotel Security. The guidelines report notes several ways in which law enforcement should coordinate with hotel security directors and staff. Not only do spectators and performers/VIPs stay in hotels, but in some cases the hotel itself is the venue (e.g., casino hotels in Las Vegas, which host world championship boxing and many other events).

Volunteers. Several law enforcement agencies expressed gratitude for large groups of volunteers—in some cases, over 1,000 individuals—who assist at major annual events. Credentialing is an issue, however, especially for access to middle or inner perimeters.

(2) Communications and Communication Technology

Radio Interoperability. For some special events, the lead agency may be able to disseminate radios on the same frequencies to all personnel involved in security. More commonly, other approaches are used to enable personnel from multiple agencies (with different radio models operating on different frequencies) to communicate in the field.

The lead agency may use advanced communications technology to link radios with different frequencies into a common communications matrix. This evolving technology acts as a networking gateway that interconnects radios with any frequencies into a common event frequency. Its effectiveness has been demonstrated at the President's Inauguration and other major events. The guidelines report also discusses (1) tips for radio communications protocol; (2) options for assigning radio channels and radio access to multiple agencies in support roles at special events; and (3) evolving technologies (e.g., wireless transmission of voice and data, use of encryption technology for radio transmissions).

Integrated Communications Command Center. One of the most important components in planning security for major special events is to develop an integrated communications command center. The integrated communications command center brings together key leaders and actors from all the agencies and jurisdictions involved in supporting security at the event. At the federal level, examples of integrated communications command centers include the DHS Joint Field Office (JFO); DHS/U.S. Secret Service's Multi-Agency Command Center (MACC); and the FBI's Joint Operations Center (JOC). On-scene coordination is most often managed in accordance with the principles of the Incident Command System (ICS), a component of the National Incident Management System (NIMS). Principles of ICS can also be applied to the operation of integrated communications command centers. The DHS NIMS Integration Center (NIC) establishes standards and training related to NIMS and ICS, and training is available through the Federal Emergency Management Agency (FEMA). NIMS is a comprehensive incident response system, developed by the Department of Homeland Security at the request of the President (Homeland Security Presidential Directive/HSPD-5). The guidelines report discusses central features of the MACC (video feeds, management system, facility requirements, contingency planning, new technologies, etc.); describes common features of ICS centers; and lists resources for more information.

(3) Access Control: Screening and Physical Security

Access control involves planning and managing security for an event's outer, middle, and inner perimeters. Outer perimeter security is used to deter vehicle traffic but not necessarily pedestrians. A key concern is vehicle bombs. Depending on the event, security may involve counter-surveillance teams, mobile field forces, and fixed posts in and around the perimeter.

Middle perimeter screening involves measures ranging from visual inspections to use of magnetometers and full pat-down searches. Issues that must be addressed include (1) the time and resources required for more stringent measures, and (2) private security v. law enforcement roles. Examples of middle perimeter challenges and solutions for such events as NFL games, the Rose Bowl, and the G-8 Summit are provided in the guidelines report.

The inner perimeter may include government officials, performers, backstage areas, etc. Screening is conducted for the proper credentials. In addition, key areas may be inspected and swept for explosives and weapons and secured long before the arrival of VIPs or spectators.

Other issues discussed in the report include:

- Use of security video cameras and alternatives/supplements (observations from raised platforms and other vantage points)

- Vulnerabilities associated with vendors and deliveries, trucks and limos, mail/express mail, and collection of cash

- Inspections of facilities and packages.

(4) Transportation/Traffic

Transportation and traffic control can make or break an event in terms of public enjoyment, but in the guidelines report the focus is on security implications—particularly, the potential for transport of explosives via any mode of transportation. Specific issues addressed include:

- Vehicle access, including unique situations where U.S. Coast Guard assistance may be needed (for example, event lodging includes cruise ships)

- Motorcades (e.g., U.S. Secret Service expertise and assistance, planning checklists)

- Importance of efficient vehicle exit flow to security and public relations

- Special traffic problems (e.g., "cruising," Mardi Gras street celebrations)

- Aircraft/helicopter access and airspace protection. The report discusses Federal Aviation Administration (FAA) temporary flight restrictions (TFRs) over certain events, especially stadiums for major sports events; security issues related to small airports; and landings of private helicopters at major special events.

(5) Intelligence

Intelligence functions—before, during, and after an event—are critical for event security. In addition to drawing on local and state intelligence resources, many law enforcement agencies receive support from the FBI's Joint Terrorism Task Forces (JTTF) and Field Intelligence Groups (FIG). The Secret Service may also assist with intelligence on dangerous subjects who have threatened public officials.

With respect to intelligence functions during events, the guidelines report briefly discusses practices related to intelligence gathering, communication, and management (e.g., scheduled intelligence briefings, field communications with intelligence experts who are stationed at communications command centers and operations centers, and investigations of tips to terrorism hotlines).

(6) Credentialing

A credential (unlike a ticket) identifies specific individuals who are allowed access to a venue for a purpose. Expenses associated with credentialing (background checks, production costs for "high tech" badges) may result in cutting corners. Sophisticated badge-making equipment and software involves placing holographs on badges, making them difficult to counterfeit. More commonly, numerical and/or color codes are used to indicate perimeter access, personnel functions, permission to carry service weapons, etc. In the future, event badges may include biometric identification and bar coding. A checklist of considerations for credentialing is included in the guidelines report.

This important function begins early in the planning phase and continues after the event. It includes obtaining adequate funding for event planning, training, payment of overtime, purchase of equipment and supplies, etc.; identifying, handling, and coordinating the needs of each subcommittee; ordering, leasing, and/or borrowing equipment; and many other details.

(7) Administrative and Logistics Support

The guidelines report discusses:

- Anticipating and working through lengthy government procurement processes for certain types of equipment.

- Exploring how other agencies—including regional councils of governments, the Federal Emergency Management Agency (FEMA), DHS Special Event program, and military special events offices—may be able to assist with equipment and supplies.

- Handling operational logistics, including personnel transport and parking; special transport and equipment needs (e.g., bicycles, generators, fences, Jersey barriers, hazmat clothing, riot gear, magnetometers); and food and beverages, bathrooms, tents for shade, and facilities/space for meetings.

- Providing administrative support—maintaining communications equipment; conducting equipment inventories; paying the bills; and many other tasks.

- Arranging for specialized support (e.g., videographers).

(8) Protecting Critical Infrastructure and Utilities

The lead agency must also coordinate with other agencies and review security plans for infrastructure and utilities that could threaten event security (local water supply, water treatment facilities, electricity supply, communications grid, sewer system, computer systems, etc.). At some special events, manhole covers have been welded shut near the event venues. Often, newspaper dispensers and public trash cans are removed before an event (they can be hiding places for bombs and can be used as missiles to harm law enforcement or destroy property). When such measures are deemed necessary, law enforcement and government officials should work with the media to alert citizens to the security justifications for the inconveniences.

(9) Fire/EMS/Hospitals/Public Health

Fire and emergency medical services (EMS) play a critical role in supporting security and public safety at special events. Additionally, hospital medical care must be adequately available if needed. Fire, EMS, and medical care should be a separate planning team, chaired by the chief fire/EMS service in the jurisdiction hosting the special event. But the plans must be integrated into the overall security plan for the event. Fire and EMS agencies will have specific needs at the event, such as stand-by and staging areas for fire apparatus, ambulances, and special operations vehicles (such as hazmat vehicles); access to critical infrastructure, e.g., sprinkler connections, fire hydrants, utility panels; and entry and egress routes for emergency vehicles.

Hospitals should also be integrated into the overall security plan in order to provide critical information to these primary health care facilities on anticipated threats and attendance to the event. Public health agencies should be included in planning sessions to assist them in preparation for potential hazmat/WMD situations that may impact the community.

(10) Hazardous Materials/Weapons of Mass Destruction: Detection, Response, and Management

In planning security for major special events, law enforcement must always consider the risk from hazardous materials and weapons of mass destruction. As discussed in this guideline, hazmat will include weapons of mass destruction. As described by the FBI, planning for hazmat incidents during special events focuses on four primary objectives: (1) availability of subject matter experts (SMEs) for rapid risk assessment of received threats, (2) procedures for venue protection from hazmat, (3) development of assessment teams for reported hazmat incidents in and around the venues, and (4) response and protective actions for law enforcement in the event of a hazmat incident. FBI protocols for these threats at major special events are described in the guideline.

The hazmat field is governed by a variety of federal regulatory agencies, including Occupational Safety and Health Administration (OSHA), Environmental Protection Agency (EPA), and Centers for Disease Control (CDC), as well as state and county agencies— state departments of homeland security, emergency management agencies, public health agencies, and others. Response to hazmat situations is also covered in the National Response Plan (NRP). Key issues for local law enforcement include:

- Deciding whether the threat to the event is great enough to acquire and employ advanced technology (e.g., radiation detectors, explosives detection devices)

- If advanced detection technology is warranted, determining whether collaborative partners, such as federal agencies, can provide the equipment and other assistance.

- Determining the level of hazmat training that should be provided to officers and supervisors, e.g., OSHA standards.

- Deciding whether to employ joint assessment teams composed of local, state, and federal subject matter experts.

A key part of hazmat planning at major special events involves developing a response plan to hazmat situations. The response plan should include measures to protect public safety; restore essential government services; and provide emergency relief to governments, businesses, and people affected by the terrorist act. Under the National Response Plan, FEMA can request resources from many other federal agencies to support local governments overwhelmed by an emergency. The Department of Homeland Security's Office of State and Local Government Coordination and Preparedness and FEMA both provide training to help local jurisdictions develop plans.*

The guidelines report notes resources that may be available to local law enforcement with respect to training; estimating the potential effects of chemical or biological agents and explosive devices; using Bureau of Alcohol, Tobacco, Firearms, and Explosives (ATF) or military explosive detection canines for national events for which the federal government has responsibility; and dealing with bomb threats (e.g., ATF protocols, checklists, forms; FBI Bomb Data Center protocols). The importance of intelligence is also discussed (information on sales or thefts of chemicals and other bomb-making materials, and on truck thefts and rentals).

Emergency Evacuation Plans. Nearly all stadiums, arenas, and other facilities holding special events will have evacuation plans for any emergency (e.g., a fire) that should have been reviewed by the fire department or fire marshal. The main responsibility of the lead security agency is to re-examine those plans and ensure they are coordinated into the overall event security plan.

*See www.ojp.usdoj.gov/odp/docs/comnet.htm and www.training.fema.gov/emiweb/terrorismInfor/termng.asp. See also National Fire Protection Association NFPA 1600: Standard on Disaster/Emergency Management and Business Continuity at www.nfpa.org/assests/files/PDF/NFPA1600.pdf.

(11) Tactical Support and Crisis Management

Depending on the nature of the event and the perceived threat level, security planners may need to engage specialized tactical units, such as SWAT (special weapons and tactics) teams, to either work the event, be on standby at an off-site location, or be on call. SWAT tactical capabilities include hostage negotiation, counter assault, counter sniper, counter surveillance, and others.

If any type of terrorist act occurs during a local special event, the FBI is the lead agency in the nation to handle terrorist responses and investigations. The FBI brings a variety of resources to deal with terrorist threats or incidents including well-trained tactical response teams, expert hostage negotiators, forensic investigators, and others.

In the event of a terrorist incident, the law enforcement response would be coordinated by the FBI in accordance with the Terrorism Incident Annex of the National Response Plan. The National Response Plan also outlines the process for requesting assistance from military resources. Another federal specialized resource available for tactical support is the ATF Special Response Team Program, which has teams based in Detroit, Los Angeles, Dallas, and Washington, D.C., available to respond anywhere in the US to conduct high-risk law enforcement operations.

(12) Public Information and Media Relations

Extensive information needs to be communicated to a variety of audiences. Public information includes (1) general information about the event—opening and performance times, parking, etc.; and (2) security information—items allowed (and not allowed) into the event, how to evacuate in an emergency, handling of protests, etc. Security planners must identify a lead coordinator for public information (e.g., city public information officer, venue media specialist, lead law enforcement agency) and the process for releasing information. The DHS has developed a useful guide as part of the National Response Plan (see, Public Affairs Support Annex). Issues addressed in the guidelines report with respect to security information include:

- Involvement of the public information coordinator in all stages of a special event

- Delivery of a consistent message about demonstration activities

- Involvement of citizens and the business community in security planning to discuss security measures that will reduce vehicle and pedestrian traffic

- Development of handbooks for officers. These may include information helpful to the public (addresses/numbers for hospitals, venues, government agencies, etc.); expectations for appearance, demeanor, and equipment; street closures; and signs of possible terrorist activity.

(13) Training

- The guidelines report provides information on training resources and issues and discusses various training approaches and areas of emphasis, including:

- Tabletop exercises, which typically involve fire/EMS, the health department/hospitals, partner law enforcement agencies, and other government officials (e.g., city/county attorney)

- Live training events where various types of terrorist attacks or other disasters are staged

- Special classes held to prepare for a specific event (rights of protestors, use of riot gear, venue security, surveillance, operating in teams, etc.)

- Training in specialized areas, such as crowd control tactics, use of hazmat/WMD or other protective equipment, etc.

- Training best practices for private venue owners.

(14) Demonstrations and Other Crowd Control Issues

Demonstrations and protests are a constant concern in some jurisdictions and a rare occurrence in others. Local police surveyed for this report varied in how (or whether) they deployed special crowd management response units. The key factors in even deploying the units were the nature of the event and the extent of the threat from protestors or possibility of celebratory disturbances. Often, they discussed crowd management in terms of taking a "soft approach at first." That is, the department did not use mobile force units as a matter of routine. Instead, crowd control officers with distinct uniforms and riot gear would be positioned in the background or were not even visible but were on duty, close by, and ready to act quickly if called upon.

In special events with obvious and stated protest movements by extremist groups who have a history of attempting to disrupt events and destroying property, law enforcement must be ready with sizeable and trained field forces capable of countering any attempts to disrupt planned events, destroy property, or break the law. In these situations, law enforcement must be prepared for mass arrest situations. The guidelines report also discusses:

- Legal support (permits, negotiations, use of force, detention, charging and arrest processing, briefings of patrol officers, and other issues)

- Restricting access (e.g., establishing protest "buffer zones")

- Planning for mass arrests

- Value of community policing in identifying and managing protesters who do not obtain permits and avoid publicity (e.g., certain self-described "anarchists")

- Role of intelligence, including collaboration with event sponsor

- Other crowd control challenges and solutions, including

    ° Prohibiting alcohol and enforcing alcohol violations

    ° Enforcing juvenile curfews

    ° Anticipating and managing gang-related problems and crimes

    ° Handling lost children.

Security Management During the Event

This phase begins as spectators, officials, crowds, media, and others begin to assemble at the event site (in some cases, days before the event begins). The guidelines report includes:

- Checklists for use immediately before and during the event in many of the responsibility areas discussed above

- Specific agenda items for personnel briefings

- Ground rules for ejection from an event and the need for law enforcement/private security agreement on these.

Post-Event Activities

After the event ends and the crowds exit, continuing responsibilities include: (1) completion of the administration and logistics plan (equipment return and inventory, removal of temporary barriers, accounting, billing, payment of overtime, etc.); and (2) debriefing and preparation of an after-action report. The guidelines report focuses on the second area and recommends:

- For multi-day events, asking supervisors to prepare daily critiques of operations so that details are not forgotten

- Conducting debriefings—interviews and/or surveys of supervisors and representatives from other law enforcement agencies and key partners (fire/EMS, city attorney, etc.)

- Preparing an after-action report that includes:

- Critiques of all operations (field operations, access points, personnel (including supervisory personnel), logistics, equipment, communications, training, etc.)

    ° Deviations from the event security plan

    ° Recommendations—what to keep, what to change, how and why changes should be made.

Office of the Director

As I have traveled around the country meeting with sheriffs, chiefs, and others in law enforcement, I am frequently reminded that in addition to all of the crime-fighting responsibilities you had before September 11, 2001, local law enforcement is now accountable for countless new responsibilities dealing with securing the homeland. These responsibilities include securing special events, being prepared for everything from disorderly conduct and vandalism to preventing and responding to acts of terrorism. Special events present unique challenges and security concerns to law enforcement, and require a great deal of planning and coordination among multiple agencies, including federal, state, and local. Events of national or regional importance attended by large numbers of people include political events, such as election rallies and conventions, and social, entertainment, and sporting events such as state fairs, concerts, and college football games. All of these events require extensive planning and management.

This guidelines report is intended to benefit agencies of all sizes that are faced with planning and managing, or participating in special event security. It provides practical recommendations and considerations for securing large-scale events, specifically, but the guidelines can be adapted for an event of any size. The strategies employed should be tailored to local circumstances and resources. As you will see in this report, community policing strategies—problem solving and partnership building—are essential to planning for and managing special events. You may find yourself partnering with federal agencies, conducting risk and threat assessments of local businesses, multiplying your force with private security, and calling on community volunteers to help make events safer and more secure for the public.

Additionally, the guidelines report benefits from the knowledge of key federal law enforcement and security experts in the Department of Homeland Security, U.S. Secret Service, Federal Bureau of Investigation, and Department of Defense. Each of these individuals and agencies has extensive experience and expertise with planning and managing special events, and in partnering with state and local law enforcement to make them a success.

I am pleased to present you with this important guidelines report. The guidelines are designed to offer examples of effective approaches used during special events handled by a variety of federal, state, and local law enforcement agencies throughout the country. I hope this report serves as a resource to you in the important work that you do every day to make our communities safer.

Sincerely,

Carl R. Peed

Director

Acknowledgments

This comprehensive project received extensive support and guidance from Carl R. Peed, Director of the Office of Community Oriented Policing Services (COPS); Timothy Quinn, Chief of Staff; Pam Cammarata, Assistant Director; Tamara Lucas, Senior Policy Analyst; Michael Seelman, Senior Social Science Analyst; Karl Bickel, Senior Policy Analyst; and other COPS staff.

Project team members included the following: (1) Institute for Law and Justice— Edward Connors (principal author), Barbara Webster, Marti Kovener, and Joan Peterschmidt; (2) Eastern Kentucky University, Department of Criminal Justice and Police Studies—Dr. Gary Cordner, Cindy Shain, Ed Brodt, Dr. Pam Collins, and Linda Mayberry; and (3) private security specialists—William Cunningham, Thomas Seamon, and Peter Ohlhausen. Hugh Nugent assisted with editing.

The project team would especially like to thank the Director and staff of the U.S. Secret Service who cooperated extensively in providing information and site observation access for this guidelines report. Extensive support was also provided by staff from the Federal Bureau of Investigation and Department of Homeland Security. We also wish to particularly thank the chief executives and event security commanders of several other agencies and companies that went out of their way to provide information and often site access that aided this report: Boston Police Department; New York City Police Department; Jacksonville (Florida) Sheriff's Office; IACP's Major Cities Chiefs; National Football League; and NASCAR.

Additionally, we thank all the professionals who gave of their time and expertise to provide information for this report. We have listed many of the key persons interviewed in Appendix A.

Table of Contents

List of Exhibits

Background

The U.S. Department of Justice Office of Community Oriented Policing Services (COPS) was directed by the Consolidated Appropriations Act, 2004, to submit a report to Congress on the "best practices" developed by various federal, state, and local law enforcement agencies to secure special events of national and regional importance. The events covered present unique security concerns for local law enforcement officials because they were to be attended by large numbers of people.sporting events, concerts, and cultural exhibitions. The COPS Office was also directed by Congress to "develop a program to train law enforcement on how to effectively secure facilities where events of national or regional importance are taking place."

The COPS Office[1] engaged the Institute for Law and Justice (ILJ),[2] a nonprofit criminal justice research organization, to assist the office in conducting a nationwide study on the best practices of law enforcement in planning and managing security for major special events. ILJ collaborated with staff from the Department of Criminal Justice and Police Studies, Eastern Kentucky University, and several private security experts to work on this project.

In developing the study approach, ILJ staff met with COPS Office staff and a number of senior officials with experience in event security and private security. The study approach included the following methodology:

- Reviewing special event security literature in journal articles, newspapers, magazines, handbooks, reports, and other materials.

- Conducting interviews with key experts in the security field including event security executives and specialists from private security firms, the National Football League, NASCAR, U.S. Secret Service, Federal Bureau of Investigation (FBI), and others.

- Conducting extensive telephone interviews with command officers from over 40 state and local law enforcement agencies regarding their experiences with planning and managing regional and national special events.

- Conducting observation visits to a number of jurisdictions to examine in depth the practices for event security including visits to the U.S. Secret Service and Boston Police Department for handling the Democratic National Convention; New York City Police Department's handling of the Republican National Convention; college football games; the Kentucky Derby; a NASCAR race; the Jacksonville (Florida) Sheriff's Office's planning for Super Bowl XXXIX; and others.

- Convening a focus group of special event security experts and obtaining technical reviews of guidelines' drafts from representatives from the Department of Homeland Security; FBI; U.S. Secret Service; Bureau of Alcohol, Tobacco, Firearms, and Explosives (ATF); local law enforcement, and the private sector to improve the guidelines.

Appendix A contains a list of the people who were interviewed and special events that were reviewed for this guidelines report.

[1] For more information, see www.cops.usdoj.gov.

[2] For more information, see www.ilj.org.

Purpose of Guidelines Report

The Guidelines for Law Enforcement on Planning and Managing Security for Major Special Events provide a framework for local law enforcement to plan and manage these unique events that draw large numbers of people to the same location for short periods of time. The guidelines are designed to offer examples of effective approaches used during key special events handled by a variety of federal, state, and local law enforcement agencies throughout the country and by private security.

The focus of the guidelines report is on major special events—events that involve regional and national importance. These are typically events that would require dedication of the greater part of an individual agency's workforce and usually involve assistance from multiple agencies. These major special events require extensive planning, elaborate communication at many levels, and a comprehensive approach.

These larger events, which often include a variety of VIPs and political figures, are also potential targets for terrorists, criminals, and protestors.

The scope of the study ranged from reviewing law enforcement security practices at the highest-level events—National Special Security Events (NSSEs)[3]—to more regional events, such as a college football game or festival that draws 75,000 people to a town with a population of 5,000. The study team spent time meeting with the two federal law enforcement agencies that are most involved in securing major special events—the Federal Bureau of Investigation and the U.S. Secret Service. The Secret Service has developed highly effective methods and approaches to major event security planning, venue and motorcade security, communications, credentialing, and training. The FBI has developed highly effective methods and approaches to the management of intelligence, crisis management, hostage rescue, and counterterrorism matters for major special events.

Although the guidelines target the larger events, they still contain information and examples that will be helpful for any law enforcement agency that is called on to plan and manage a special event of any size. For these smaller special events, law enforcement may pick and choose from practical recommendations throughout the report that may apply to their unique event, particularly if there are resource limitations. As one special events commander noted, "It is better to be over-prepared than under-prepared for a special event."

As another law enforcement special events commander noted, when events are produced year after year, departments already have a security plan ("template") for the event, and they benefit from longstanding organizational relationships with sponsors and other agencies. Even so, she commented, "continual fine-tuning of the plan is required in light of changes in personnel assignments, resources, the nature of potential threats, event activities, performers/speakers, and other changes."

The guidelines are intended to be adaptable to a variety of circumstances and special events. Law enforcement does not want a "one size fits all" solution to handling special events. Too many situations are unique. These guidelines involve a variety of examples and approaches that can be tailored to individual special events. These are general guidelines, and local jurisdictions must decide how to apply them to their local conditions given available resources.

In developing these guidelines, we do not wish to needlessly alarm law enforcement across the U.S. that the annual county fair that has been held in mid-America for 100 years is now a terrorist target. However, as First Deputy Commissioner Patricia Giorgio-Fox, Philadelphia Police Department, commented during this study:

> Pre-9/11, special event management primarily concerned crowd and traffic issues. Post-9/11, homeland security and domestic preparedness issues outweigh crowd and traffic issues.

[3] In 1998, the President issued Presidential Decision Directive 62, which delineated the roles and responsibilities of federal agencies in developing and implementing security plans for major events. When an event is designated a National Special Security Event by the Department of Homeland Security, after consultation with the Homeland Security Counsel, the U.S. Secret Service assumes the role as the lead agency for the design and implementation of the operational security plan, the FBI is the lead agency for crisis management, and FEMA is the lead agency for consequence management. Key NSSEs from 2002 through 2004 have included the Olympics at Salt Lake City, 2002 Super Bowl, President's State of the Union Address, Democratic and Republican National Conventions, G-8 Summit, and others.

[4] The 9/11 Commission Report, Final Report of the National Commission on Terrorist Attacks upon the United States, 2004, p. 339.

One of the key messages from the 9/11 Commission Report was that "We believe the 9/11 attacks revealed four kinds of failures: in imagination, policy, capabilities, and management."[4] In terms of imagination, we can no longer safely say, "It can't happen here." In terms of policy, governing bodies need to become more actively involved in assessing the need for special event security. In terms of capabilities, all law enforcement should be ratcheting up its capabilities to prevent and respond to terrorist threats and attacks—the homegrown terrorists, like Timothy McVeigh, are as much a threat as Al Qaeda. In terms of management, becoming better organized and improving communication and cooperation among agencies also helps them deal better with their day-to-day mission of preventing and responding to everyday crime and natural disasters.

Local law enforcement agencies should think about planning for major special event security from a community policing perspective.[5] Community policing strategies such as problem solving and partnership building may be effective law enforcement tools. As Professor Geoffrey Alpert and Chief Dan Flynn note in a case study of securing Super Bowl XXXIII:

> The complex demands of special event security often require the police department to organize and train a special unit. Large events or events occurring in certain areas may require the efforts of several departmental units or different local, regional, state, or federal agencies. Therefore, major sporting events, musical performances, festivals and ceremonies involving world leaders and the like, which attract tens of thousands of people, easily qualify as "communities" for the purpose of policing. The Super Bowl is one of the biggest events in American sports. The philosophical, strategic, tactical and organizational dimensions of community policing[6] can be practically applied to its planning. (Alpert 2000).

A recent publication by the COPS Office shows how community policing strategies are connected to preventing and responding to terrorism.[7] A key passage from the publication notes:

> For the past 20 years, community policing has encouraged law enforcement to partner with the community to proactively identify potential threats and create a climate of safety. Its emphasis on problem solving has led to more effective means of addressing crime and social disorder problems. In the 21st Century, the community policing philosophy is well positioned to take a central role in preventing and responding to terrorism and in efforts to reduce citizen fear. Law enforcement agencies should realize that community policing is more important than ever in proactively dealing with and responding to terrorism in their jurisdictions.

The guidelines focus most on special events that involve public law enforcement in the planning and implementation of security for spectators and the public. But there are many events, especially concerts, that are planned and managed by the private sector. In many of these events, the private management company also manages the security. Public law enforcement may not be involved at all in these events, unless called to the scene to handle disturbances or crimes.

[5] See COPS Office's definition of Community Policing at www.cops.usdoj.gov/Default.asp?Item=36.

[6] See Cordner, Gary. *Community Policing: Elements and Effects. In Critical Issues in Policing: Contemporary Readings,* edited by R. Dunham and G. Alpert. Prospect Heights, Illinois: Waveland Press, 1997

[7] See www.cops.usdoj.gov/mime/open.pdf?Item=1046.

Guiding Principles for Major Special Events Security

Below are some guiding principles for law enforcement for planning and managing security for major special events:

- Ensure that timely and effective planning, communication, and training are prioritized. Jurisdictions handling special events on a routine basis should consider building events security training into basic and in-service training.

- Understand that overall management of special events is temporary—it involves developing new organizational arrangements, new relationships, and new structures. It is like managing a multi-agency temporary organization. As Professor Jack Green noted in the report on the Salt Lake City Olympics, "The key challenge in this context is to forge new relationships in a time-limited way that can bridge difficult challenges. This may be the key challenge in the entire safety and security operation." (Greene 2002).

- Plan for and manage for the worst-case scenarios—extraordinary crime (and depending on the event, extreme protestors' activities) and possible terrorist attack—but really be prepared to deal with the most ordinary and mundane crimes (pickpockets, thefts from autos, and vandalism) and common civil disruptions (fighting, drunkenness, and disorderly conduct).

- Anticipate unplanned activities and spur of the moment gatherings, for example, on the eve of a major event (Super Bowl, World Series game).

- Secure all perimeters including those in outer areas. In large special events, law enforcement must secure a series of perimeters (inner, middle, and outer). These often involve specific facilities and well-defined territorial venues. However, law enforcement must also be responsible for safety and security in the "theater"—the broader "unbounded" areas of the city or county where other events may occur or VIPs stay in hotels. (Greene, 2002).

- Realize that law enforcement needs to be concerned not only with the safety and security of participants and the event venue, but also the economics of the event. Many events involve commerce, have a budget, and provide income to the local economy.

- Recognize the need for and benefits of leveraging resources and collaborating with other law enforcement agencies; federal agencies; public safety (fire/EMS); other city, county, and state agencies (health, building codes, transportation, parks & recreation); and private security.

- Develop an effective interoperable communications capability if multiple agencies are involved in the field.

- Involve citizens and the business community in planning efforts.

- Ensure that the event continues safely and at the same time respect Constitutional rights including freedom of speech and assembly.

- Ensure that the rest of the jurisdiction receives essential law enforcement services, regardless of the size or importance of the event.

- Evaluate continuously and review operations and practices to update and improve security. Prepare an after-action report after each event.

- Ensure that appropriate federal officials, such as DHS State Homeland Security Advisors, are informed in advance about events with national or international significance to guarantee federal awareness and possible support.

This guidelines report is not all-inclusive. It presents state and local law enforcement with the highlights of special event security planning and management. There are obviously many more procedural and technical details involved in each area presented in the report. The document also contains helpful resources to turn to for more detail.

Overview of Process for Planning and Managing Major Special Events

Special event security planning and implementation involves three phases:

- Pre-Event Planning: This phase should begin 12-18 months before the date of the event, depending on the nature of the event. This phase involves the lead agency receiving authorization, establishing its mission, reaching out to collaborate with other partners to help secure the event, meeting regularly with team members and partners, and developing detailed security plans and contingency plans.

- Security Management during the Event: This phase begins just before spectators, officials, crowds, media, and others begin to assemble at the event sites. For some events (e.g., Super Bowl, NASCAR races, conventions), people begin to gather days prior to the actual event or game. This phase includes comprehensive communications, monitoring, and reporting. It involves ensuring that key operational areas are functioning properly, such as the communications command center, credentialing, access control posts, and more. It also involves checking on the readiness of field and support areas such as mobile field forces to deal with crowd control, intelligence support, arrest processing, EMS/medical support, and more.

- Post-Event Activities: This phase, which begins when the event is over, includes conducting a comprehensive review of the successes and areas needing improvement concerning event security. It also involves accounting for all equipment and other resources used, including paying bills for the security.

Each of these phases will be discussed in more detail throughout this report.

Pre-Event Planning

> The secret of getting ahead is getting started. The secret of getting started is breaking your complex overwhelming tasks into small manageable tasks, and then starting on the first one.
>
> *Mark Twain*

For most of the major special events studied for this report, law enforcement agencies began planning over a year prior to the event. Agencies must have adequate time to study assignments, build alliances and partnerships, obtain adequate equipment and technology, conduct training, and more.

However, some events, like President Reagan's memorial service shortly after his death, don't allow as much advance planning. For these events, law enforcement must rely on its professionalism, partnerships, and previous experience handing related events.

Bringing in other law enforcement agencies to provide event security on short notice depends on previously cultivated relationships, a hallmark of community policing.

The key areas that must be dealt with in the early stages of planning for the special event include creating the mission or charter, clarifying event security leadership, developing partnership agreements, resolving legal authority issues, and developing the planning organization structure and assignments. Each area will be discussed below.

Mission/Charter

Law enforcement should clarify the mission and receive a written charter or authorization from the legal authority for the jurisdiction—Governor, Mayor, City Manager—before developing plans to secure a special event. For example, in a recent event studied, the commission created to oversee the event wrote that the local police had the following mission: Make the event successful—enjoyable for participants, but also safe and secure.

This helps to clarify law enforcement's objective in applying security measures and approaches. The message for this event was that if the security was too restrictive, the event could be safe but not enjoyable for participants. For example, if participants were extensively screened to enter the event facility and long waiting lines developed, the event overseers would not consider this a desired outcome.

In order to avoid confusion and meet the desired outcomes of the event authorities, law enforcement should clarify the security mission and ask for a written charter.

As a recent example, the Master Agreement between the City of Boston and the Democratic National Convention Committee obligated the city to provide law enforcement and public safety services to the convention facility (Fleet Center), the DNC headquarters hotel, delegates' hotels, and other venues holding DNC-related activities.[8] To fulfill this legal obligation, the Boston Police Department developed the following mission statement in its Operational Plan:

> During the convention period, the Department has two primary and supporting missions. The first is to provide 24-hour police services to the residents of the City's neighborhoods. The goal of this mission is to prevent crime, maintain order, and provide services to the City's residents and visitors to our City. The Department's second mission is to provide security to DNC facilities and events, and protect participants to the Convention. In furtherance of this mission, the Department is to facilitate cooperation, and coordinate the activities of other City Departments, County, State, and federal agencies to provide a level of public safety services that ensures the safety, and an atmosphere of hospitality, for all individuals attending or participating in DNC events.

Of course, this requires the governing bodies to define special events that require special law enforcement attention to security. For example, the Department of Homeland Security defines a National Special Security Event (NSSE) as a designated domestic or international event that, by virtue of its profile or status, represents a significant target, and therefore warrants additional preparation, planning, and mitigation efforts. In its Special Events Management Planning Handbook, the FBI defines a special event as:

> A significant domestic or international event, occurrence, circumstance, contest, activity, or meeting, which by virtue of its profile and/or status represents an attractive target for terrorist attack.

*The Democratic National Convention was designated a National Special Security Event by the Department of Homeland Security. The U.S. Secret Service was designated as the lead agency to coordinate security at the DNC.

Clarify Leadership Authority and Structure

The charter should also clarify which law enforcement agency has legal and leadership authority and responsibility to control the security of the event, and define what the role of assisting agencies is. In planning and managing major special events, there is a critical need to identify which agency is in charge—the centralized command and control—having legal and financial control and responsibility for securing the event.

Governing bodies must define events that require the highest levels of law enforcement attention to security. For example, the Secretary of DHS, after consultation with the Homeland Security Counsel, is responsible for designating National Special Security Events (NSSE). NSSEs are significant domestic or international events, which, by virtue of their profile or status, represent a significant target, and warrant additional preparation, planning and mitigation efforts. By definition, an NSSE is an Incident of National Significance as defined by the National Response Plan.

By Presidential directive, the U.S. Secret Service is the lead agency for the design and implementation of the operational security plan for the NSSE. The FBI is the lead federal agency for crisis management, counterterrorism, hostage rescue, and intelligence, and the Federal Emergency Management Agency (FEMA) is the lead federal agency for consequence management (response and recovery operations).

The DHS Special Event Working Group (SEWG) uses the role of a Federal Coordinator (FC) to enable federal support to appropriately-designated special events that are under state and local jurisdiction and to coordinate federal incident management and security assistance activities including prevention, preparedness, response, and recovery, as appropriate. Designated by the Secretary of Homeland Security, the FC serves as the Secretary's representative locally and is the principal federal point of contact for facilitating coordination of federal support with state, local, and private sector event planners and participating Federal Departments.

In the Salt Lake City Olympics, state legislation established the Utah Olympic Public Safety Command, which became part of the Department of Public Safety (chaired by the Commissioner of Public Safety) to oversee and coordinate the event. In contrast, many special events are held on privately owned property. During a Washington Red-skins National Football League game, which draws over 90,000 spectators to FedEx Field in Lanham, Maryland, leadership is shared among the stadium owner, the Prince George's County Police Department, and the Fire Department, depending on the nature of the decision that has to be made. It is important to clarify the legal relationships and leadership of event security forces in order to avoid issues and delays when it comes time to make important public safety decisions regarding the event.

Develop Partnership Agreements

Security demands for many major special events require more personnel resources than the lead agency can afford to assign—the agency must also continue to provide adequate resources to police the city or county as usual. It is not unusual to have a variety of federal, state, and local law enforcement agencies working together to secure a major special event. During the World War II Memorial commemoration event, the U.S. Park Police and Metropolitan DC Police Department were assisted by 32 law enforcement agencies from Virginia, New Jersey, New York, and Pennsylvania, in addition to the U.S. Secret Service, FBI, U.S. Marshals Service, ATF, and other federal agencies. In the G-8 Summit held on Sea Island, Georgia, in June 2004, which was designated an NSSE, the U.S. Secret Service was assisted by 20,000 sworn law enforcement officers from over 130 different federal, state, and local agencies.

10

Even for regional special events—a city's July 4th or Mardi Gras—where local police do not routinely call in other law enforcement agencies, although the state police may assist with traffic and the sheriff's office may increase staff to handle anticipated arrests, other local law enforcement agencies may still be on standby for these events, for example, to provide tactical officers if the need arises.

In these multiple agency situations, it is useful to develop a memorandum of understanding (MOU) or Memorandum of Agreement (MOA) between the lead agency and the assisting agencies. The MOU should be simple, brief, and straightforward. The objective is to memorialize roles and responsibilities, not create burdensome paperwork. The MOU should accomplish the following:

- Clarify the legal authority of the assisting agency to enforce the law in the lead agency's jurisdiction, if needed (see section below).

- Enumerate the commitment of the assisting agency in providing personnel resources and equipment (radios, vehicles, etc.).

- Clarify when and where the assisting agency's officers should arrive and the specifics of their assignments (e.g., duty posts, shifts, roles, etc.).

- Clarify any compensation for labor costs, expenses (e.g., gas, food and beverages, hotel, supplies, etc.), and equipment costs incurred by the assisting agency.

It is also important to partner with the private sector. This includes businesses that will be affected by the special event and private security, which is often involved in securing events on private property. The private sector has many resources that can be used effectively in securing special events. For example, Phoenix, Arizona, police give a great deal of credit for successful special events to the Downtown Phoenix Partnership, a non-profit corporation that serves residents, fans, visitors, and downtown employees. Police meet regularly with the Partnership on special events issues affecting Copper Square, a 92-square-block area that hosts Major League Baseball, professional basketball, and many other events. The downtown operations unit commander explained that the police department was able to work effectively and communicate all safety and traffic issues with the Partnership for the 2001 World Series. The commander noted "this was a major success with millions of eyes on downtown Phoenix just weeks after the tragic events on September 11."

Security planning and management for the San Diego County Fair involves a partnership between the San Diego County Sheriff's Department and the 22nd Agricultural District, a state agency that owns the Fairground property. About 1.2 million people attended the 2004 event over 11 days. The Sheriff's Office assigns a dozen or more officers with supervisors to work on site daily, as well as a separate traffic enforcement detail. The Fairgrounds uses a private security company year round (Del Mar Race Track is also located there), and other private security companies are hired to work the county fair event.

Communication with the business community is critical. Although representatives of retail, restaurant, and other small businesses may not be at security planning meetings, in planning special event security, police often talk with them about what to expect, discuss potential problems, or review the law about alcohol service to intoxicated individuals.

Bringing other city agencies in as partners is also critical. The obvious agencies include fire, emergency medical services, transportation, sanitation, code enforcement, and others. These agencies have resources and roles to play in securing special events. For example, the transit company in Austin, Texas, has trained 13 police officers to drive city buses. The company now "turns over the keys" to police to use the buses for special events—for example, to transport equipment and officers to their posts.

Developing and maintaining the above types of partnerships with other law enforcement and public safety agencies, other city and county agencies, private security, the business community, and neighborhoods should be natural activities for police agencies that have been practicing community policing strategies throughout the years.

Legal Authority of Assisting Agencies

In multiple agency major special events, it is important to clarify the legal authority of the assisting agencies early in the planning process. The assisting agencies often need to be granted temporary legal authority to enforce laws in the lead agency's jurisdiction.

This temporary law enforcement power also allows the assisting agencies to be cloaked within the same law enforcement immunities, privileges, and legal protections as the lead agency.

When the lead event security agency is a federal agency, such as with the World War II Memorial commemoration event, the U.S. Marshals Service has authority to deputize all participating law enforcement agencies to enforce law on federal lands. For the recent G-8 Summit, the local law enforcement officers from some jurisdictions in Georgia and some other states lacked legal authority to enforce the law throughout Georgia until the Governor issued an executive order authorizing the Georgia Bureau of Investigation's Director to swear them in as temporary special agents of the state.

While many jurisdictions had signed mutual aid pacts to assist each other in emergencies in the Boston area, these agreements were strictly construed to mean "emergencies," such as fires and natural disasters (floods). Thus, these existing agreements were not useful when the Boston Police Department needed assistance from dozens of outside law enforcement agencies to help secure the Democratic National Convention in June 2004. The Boston Police Department still needed help from the local county sheriff to deputize the outside law enforcement officers, military personnel, National Guard, and others.

It is also important to plan for the logistics of the swearing in of hundreds or thousands of outside agency personnel, if the state law requires an "in-person" ceremony. In some cases, such as with an event with a short duration (e.g., Inauguration) it may be advisable to bring all the officers together in a large facility (e.g., school gym) and deputize them all at once. However, in other cases, such as events lasting several days, officers may have to be deputized in shifts as they first arrive to work for their initial assignments (if officers were being paid overtime, it would be cost prohibitive to bring them all together at one time). In some jurisdictions, the process can be completed by telephone or document when necessary.

Exhibit 1. Major Special Event Security Key Functional Areas	
• Personnel resources	• Training
• Tactical support/crisis managment	• Prisoner processing
• Emergency evacuation	• Fire/EMS/hospital services
• Transportation/traffic	• Airspace security
• HAZMAT/WMD	• Intelligence
• Communications: interagency/technical	• Legal issues
• Consequence managment	• Budget and logistics
• Managing disorder Intelligence	• Field operations/venue security
• Media relations/PR	• Critique—after-action evaluation
• Critical infrastructure/utilities	• Credentialing

Lead Agency Organization for Planning and Managing the Major Special Event

The first action for the lead event security agency is to appoint the event security director or coordinator. Depending on the size and complexity of the event, this should be a dedicated assignment until the event is completed. Many larger law enforcement agencies also have a permanent special events coordinator position.

One important lesson for law enforcement was learned from the 1999 World Trade Organization (WTO) conference protestor riots in Seattle. The Seattle Police Department's After Action Report recommended that for major special events, such as a WTO meeting, the planning model should include:

> Dedicated fulltime planning personnel representing the impacted agencies; written agreements, memoranda and contracts defining all deployment and operations; and an integrated review process for decisions concerning planning, deployment, and command.[9]

[9]See Seattle Police Department, After Action Report, World Trade Organization Ministerial Conference, November 29- December 3, 1999.

The security director should be authorized to oversee the development and implementation of all security plans for the event. The director should have the authority to negotiate and sign MOUs for assistance provided by other agencies. The size and magnitude of the special event also dictates whether the event security director reports directly to the chief executive of the lead agency or to an assistant or deputy to the executive.

Early in the planning stages, the lead agency should develop a detailed organization chart for planning and managing the major special event. This will help clarify assignments, roles, and responsibilities for the event within the lead agency. This organization chart will also list the chain of command for each assignment. The chart will break the event down into responsibility areas (see Exhibit 1).

There are a variety of organizational arrangements depending on the size of the special event, number of outside agencies participating, various locations of the event, level of VIPs, threat assessments, planned protest movements, and more. The main point of creating an organizational chart is to make sure that all key responsibility areas are assigned and everyone knows with whom to communicate on all aspects of security for the event. This will be helpful not only to the lead agency, but also to all participating agencies, other agencies in the jurisdiction, and businesses, citizens, and government officials involved in the event.

Two examples of major special event organization charts are found in Appendix C. These charts have been condensed from the originals, which included more detail. The names of the officials have also been removed from the charts.

The key functional areas that should be designated for major special event security planning purposes also vary by event. Since the larger events have more detail, resources, and time, they typically have more functional areas so the detail can be planned better. Smaller events condense many of the functions together because they cannot afford to have too many people involved in planning activities. Some of the more typical functional responsibility areas are shown below. Some agencies also use slightly different terminology than others.

One of the best models for creating a major special event planning structure is the framework used by the U.S. Secret Service. This model, which includes an executive committee and detailed functional subcommittees, has been improved on over the years and is now used for all NSSEs.

Most major special event planning begins with the creation of the executive steering committee or team, headed by the overall event security director. This is typically the top command level personnel from all the key agencies that will be partners in securing the event. These partners meet initially, hopefully at least 12-18 months in advance for major special events, to agree to MOUs and approve the planning framework and process for the event. This team guides and oversees the development of the event operational plan. Some of the issues that the executive steering committee decides include: (1) identifying any other agencies including law enforcement, fire, EMS, state, federal, etc., that should be part of the special event security operation; and (2) enumerating each of the functional areas that need to be planned. In doing this, they create subcommittees (and select chairs or cochairs) and issue timelines—who will plan what by when.

The first order of business for the new planning subcommittees is to meet and develop task statements and meeting schedules. Members should have alternates in case they miss meetings. Each subcommittee should also take minutes of the meetings—who attended, what was discussed, and what was decided. These minutes provide an historical record of event plans and agency agreements. The minutes should be taken electronically so they can be e-mailed as needed. The minutes should be forwarded to the overall event security director.

Each planning subcommittee, which may involve personnel from different agencies, will meet as much as needed to develop the functional area plans. These team meetings: (1) build support for the plans, (2) pinpoint areas of needs, (3) build relationships and camaraderie, and (4) create trust. Superintendent Robert Dunford, Boston Police Department, in charge of the agency's security for the 2004 Democratic National Convention, asked each of his planning subcommittees to answer the following questions:

- What do you have in terms of personnel, equipment, and other resources?

- What do you need?

- How do you recommend getting what you need?

- What help do you need?

- What is the proposed security plan for your functional responsibility?

Once subcommittee plans are developed, the event security director and steering committee review them. The purpose of their review is to determine if the subcommittee plans are comprehensive, consistent, and realistic. There will also be an administrative review by governing bodies, such as attorneys and accountants, if they are not already part of the steering committee. This review will consider questions such as: How do event operational plans impact everyday policies and procedures of the law enforcement agency and other jurisdictional agencies? Do we need to make temporary changes in any routine policies, practices, or laws? For example, one city had to implement an emergency clause in the union contract to change officer schedules to work 12-hour shifts for the major special event.

The executive committee must also continue to update and modify plans as needed—as conditions or exposures may change right up to the date of the special event. In addition, all plans should have contingency plans—to cover the "what if" scenarios.

The most obvious need for planning security of major special events is staffing. However, it is worth stressing that early in the planning process, the planning teams should identify any equipment that will need to be purchased. Agencies have learned over the years that it takes months to order and receive shipment on some equipment. At the G-8 Summit in Georgia, some law enforcement officers had to go through training exercises without the crowd control equipment that was ordered and shipped late.

An important point made by an experienced special events commander was that law enforcement should build the use of special events equipment into normal police work—all equipment should be dual use—so that it wouldn't need to be specially ordered for the event.

It is also important to plan for turnover in subcommittee leadership. As major special events are planned 12-18 months ahead of the event, and most of the planning leadership positions are filled by senior command staff, some of these people may retire before the event is held. In addition, as agencies found in the Boston Democratic National Convention and the Salt Lake City Olympics, other officers in key planned assignments may get transferred or promoted before the event is held. Thus, turnover in key responsibility positions must be planned for.

Conduct Threat and Risk Assessments

Early in the major special event planning process, law enforcement needs to conduct a comprehensive threat and risk assessment regarding the special event in order to plan for possible situations. First Deputy Commissioner Patricia Giorgio-Fox of the Philadelphia Police Department stresses the importance of conducting threat assessments for special events:

> Special event planning now always takes into consideration the possibility of a catastrophic event. The worst-case scenario is much worse since 9/11, and it is more conceivable. Threat assessments are now done before all special events.

This section of the guideline provides examples from federal agencies and the private sector on developing assessment tools. State and local agencies should use these examples to develop tools that fit their own unique special events.

Major special events can also be categorized by predetermined rating scales to help agencies assess the level of support and resources that an event may require. This is similar to the Department of Homeland Security's "Homeland Security Advisory System," which assigns one of five codes—low/green through severe/red—based on the risk of terrorist attack. These threat assessments allow agencies to take appropriate protective measures to prevent terrorist attacks and secure critical infrastructure.

Currently, the FBI, in its Special Events Planning & Procedures Handbook, analyzes the following factors to assess Special Event Readiness Levels (SERL) to determine how much FBI support is appropriate for a major special event.

1. Size of the event (and resources available in the field office).

2. Threat—includes known threats to the event, current levels of domestic and global terrorist activities, and the realistic degree of danger that known terrorist groups may pose to the event.

3. Significance—some events have historical, political, and/or symbolic significance that may heighten concerns about the event being a target.

4. Duration—events lasting for extended periods of time require more resources.

5. Location—certain locations may be more inviting for attacks; the geographic dispersion of an event is also a factor.

6. Attendance—who is attending (cultural, political, and religious backgrounds).

7. Media coverage—events with national or international media coverage may provide an inviting stage with a large audience for attackers to make a "statement."

8. Dignitaries—high-level heads of state and VIPs require more protection and resources because they are targets for attacks.

The FBI uses the above factors to classify special events into four SERLs—Level I (full support of U.S. government personnel) through Level IV (minimal support by U.S. government personnel—state and local resources are adequate). This system may be changed in the future as the FBI begins using the new Special Event Assessment Rating (SEAR).

The Department of Homeland Security developed classifications for Special Event Homeland Security Levels (SEHSs). The highest priority security special event is designated an NSSE, which has been described earlier. Below that level, there are SEHS Level 1 (high threat level: event of large national or international importance requiring significant Federal support, e.g., the Super Bowl) through SEHS Level 4 (minimal threat level—no need for Federal support).

The federal-level interagency Special Event Working Group is in the process of revising the separate special event readiness levels used by DHS and the FBI. This revised system will be referred to as the Special Event Assessment Rating (SEAR). The SEAR will unite the current SERL (FBI) and SEHS (DHS) systems in order to eliminate the duplication and confusion that results from having two different special event rating systems. The SEAR incorporates a risk methodology that prioritizes special events submitted to the federal government for their awareness and consideration of support. The system uses seven factors in its risk assessment process to arrive at five Special Event Assessment Rating levels (e.g., SEAR-I: full U.S. Government support to SEAR-V: require state and local resources). The seven factors are:

- General Attendance–number of general public attendees

- Dignitary Attendance–number of VIPs and high-level heads of state in attendance

- Significance–historic, political, religious, and/or symbolic significance (that might make the event a more attractive target)

- Venue Site–dispersion of the site and protective complexity

- Duration–temporal considerations that may effect resource allocations

- Location–certain locations may be more inviting for an attack(s)

- Preparedness–state/local ability to protect an event

The International Association of Assembly Managers (IAAM)[10] recommends a four-tiered system for establishing threat levels at special events. Exhibit 2 illustrates the corresponding relationships between the DHS Homeland Security Advisory System and special event venue threat levels.

[10] Center for Venue Management Studies, *IAAM Safety and Security Task Force Best Practices Planning Guide: Convention Centers/ Exhibit Halls.* International Association of Assembly Managers, Inc. 2002.

Exhibit 2. IAAM's Suggested Risk Levels at Special Events				
DHS Rating	Risk Level	Venue Threat	Security Measures	Action Steps
Severe	5	Cancel	Secured	"Lock down" patrol perimeters restricting access
High	4	Maximum	Government Control	National law officials/security agencies screen public and take control
Elevated	3	Elevated	Restrictive	May involve regional or local law officials with "pat down" measures
Guarded	2	Moderate	Protective	Limited access to venue with screening precautions implemented
Low	1	Minimum	Routine	No primary factors of concern exist outside normal routine measures

[11] *Vulnerability Assessment Methodologies Report*, Office of Domestic Preparedness, U.S. Department of Homeland Security, July 2003.

[12] See also Chipley, M. and M. Kaminskas. *Building Design for Homeland Security: Providing Protection to People and Buildings* (Publication E 155), January 2004, FEMA, www.fema.gov/txt/fima/155/e155_sm.txt.

[13] W. Dean Lee, Risk "Assessments and Future Challenges," *FBI Law Enforcement Bulletin*, Vol. 74, No. 7, July 2005, pgs. 1-13.

Conducting a comprehensive threat and risk assessment of a major special event involves (1) identifying potential threats—common crimes (robbery, assault, etc.); fires; vandalism; natural disasters (earthquakes, flooding, tornados); protestors; terrorism; gangs; (2) gauging potential damages from such threats (impact analysis); (3) determining the likelihood of these threats occurring; and (4) developing cost estimates and actions to prevent the threats.

There are various methods involved in conducting threat and risk assessments. For example, the DHS' Vulnerability Assessment Methodologies Report[11] contains examples for conducting threat and risk assessments to employ effective security plans.[12] The DHS report expresses risk as an equation:

Risk = Consequences x Likelihood

Likelihood of occurrence is further defined as threat (any indication, circumstance, or event with the potential to cause loss or damage to an asset—taking into account the intention and capability of an adversary) times vulnerability (a weakness that can be exploited by an adversary to gain access to an asset, e.g., building characteristics, security practices, personal behaviors, etc.).

The FBI's Security Risk Analysis staff has also developed the analytical risk management (ARM) process to calculate assets, threats, vulnerabilities, and risks associated with security for events or programs.[13]

The U.S. Secret Service has also developed threat assessment tools, primarily regarding protecting targets.[14] However, as Alexander Berlonghi notes in his special event risk management manual, "there is quite a difference in performing a risk analysis in the special event environment as opposed to other workplaces." Since special events are not set up until a few days prior to the event, it is often difficult to get an accurate picture of what the event will look like, exactly who and how many people will attend, and other factors. "You don't have the opportunity of seeing everyone in action with all the spectators present." (Berlonghi, 1994).

The main threat and risk categories include: (1) injuries or harm to persons, such as spectators, VIPs, vendors, agency staff, and bystanders; (2) damage to property including buildings, equipment, machinery, vehicles, personal possessions, etc.; (3) loss of revenue for event and jurisdiction because of incidents that prevent people from attending or increase expenses to deal with the incident; (4) increased liability due to negligence; and (5) loss of reputation—tourists may not come to the jurisdiction or event again because of problems.

It makes sense to begin with obvious threats: common crimes, vandalism, protestor disruptions, fires, power outages, and other natural disasters (e.g., for the Salt Lake City Olympic games, they planned for a bad snowstorm; a tornado hit during a Tulsa State Fair; and there was a public suicide attempt during Riverfest in Cincinnati one year—an individual threatened to jump from a bridge). As information and intelligence comes in, plan for more serious threats. Then create appropriate security measures to deal with likely potential threats. Develop a series of worst-case scenarios—and plans to mitigate the problems and issues that arise in each case.

For police agencies that have been practicing community-policing strategies, conducting special event threat assessments relies on the same principles and practices as problem identification, analyses, and developing response plans.[15] Police agencies should also be familiar with the principles and practices of Crime Prevention Through Environmental Design/CPTED (Crowe, 2000). CPTED strategies help law enforcement analyze and incorporate environmental settings, including major event facilities, downtown streets, and parking areas, to deter crime and disorder.

Police agencies should also develop partnerships with private sector security managers who may help provide information for threat assessments. The private sector should also be recipients of law enforcement's threat assessment information, where private sector facilities might be targets.

[14] See Fein, Robert and Bryan Vossekull, National Institute of Justice, Washington, D.C., July 1998, www.ustreas.gov/usss/ntac/ntac_pi_guide_state.pdf and Borum, et al., "Threat Assessment: Defining an Approach for Evaluating Risk of Targeted Violence," *Behavioral Sciences & the Law*, 17: 323-337, 1999, John Wiley and Sons.

[15] See Scheider et al, *Connecting the Dots for a Proactive Approach*, Office of Community Oriented Policing Services, U.S. Department of Justice, p. 161, www.cops.usdoj.gov/mime/open.pdf?Item=1046.

General guidelines for performing the information collection phase of a threat and risk assessment of a major special event include:

- Assign responsibility for the assessment to an experienced and qualified assessor. In smaller events, this may be a one-person assignment. For major events, the executive team may ask each subcommittee to conduct its own assessment in its area of responsibility. Provide timelines for assessment reports.

- Obtain and review available information. This includes facility plansfloor plans, diagrams, utility layouts, electrical, etc.); photos of the geographic area (maps, aerial photos); reports from previous events; agreements or contracts signed by the governing body with event staff; certificates of insurance; inspection reports of the facilities (fire, health, safety); existing facility evacuation and emergency plans; facility or event policies, rules, and regulations; list of assets and value; and more.

- Assess the security plans of key event hotels. Interview hotel security staff for plans. For Super Bowl XXXIX, the Jacksonville Sheriff's Office was responsible for security of five cruise ships that were docked around the city and used as hotels and celebration venues.

- Conduct extensive site observations and surveys. Identify all venues, traffic routes, facilities, grounds, parking areas, etc., that need to be secured and protected. Examine the layouts at different times of the day (light, dark) and days of the week to observe varying traffic and pedestrian patterns. What impact will the event have on normal traffic and pedestrian patterns, rush hour, parking, etc.? Identify vulnerabilities. For example, the Technical Support Working Group has developed a set of guidelines that estimate the effects of a bomb on a structure and personnel in the structure.[16]

- Examine all forms of transportation that participants will use to travel to the event—airports, trains, buses, subways, etc. Identify vulnerabilities. For the 2004 Democratic National Convention in Boston, the city (with approval from the state and federal government) closed Interstate 93, which runs next to the Convention Center (Fleet Center), while the event was active, and also closed the Massachusetts Bay Transit Authority's North Station that runs under the Fleet Center.[17]

- Conduct interviews with key event planners in the governing jurisdiction and the event promoters. An event such as the Super Bowl will include early negotiations among the host city officials, NFL officials, local NFL team owners, stadium authority, key vendors, selected hotels, and others. All these people have ideas and plans for the event. It is important to obtain their plans early on.

- Obtain threat intelligence information from intelligence sources. This may include the lead agency's own intelligence resources but should also include requesting information from the state police or state bureau of identification and the local FBI Joint Terrorism Task Force (JTTF) and Field Intelligence Group (FIG).

- Develop detailed participant profiles. Identify the full range of participants planned for the event in terms of dignitaries, VIPs, event staff, government officials, performers, spectators, media, protestors, etc. Identify any cultural, religious, and political aspects of participants that may be relevant to security.

[17] These decisions were based on blast analyses conducted by the Department of Defense. In contrast, during the Republican National Convention in New York City, the train station under the convention center (Madison Square Garden) was not closed because the blast analysis showed minimal likelihood of penetration to the convention center floor.

[16] See TSWG at www.tswg.gov/tswg/prods_pubs/CardSetPress.htm.

One of the most important guidelines to remember, as noted in the DHS Vulnerability Assessment Methodologies Report, is that the "quality and diligence of the assessor is as important, or more important, than the specific methodology used."

The DHS Risk Management Division (RMD) is developing on-line Vulnerability Identification Self-Assessment Tools (ViSATs).[18] The initial modules are designed for use by stadium, arena, convention center, performing arts center, and speedway managers. Modeled after a self-assessment tool used by the Transportation Security Administration (TSA), completing the on-line forms raises the public facility manager's security awareness levels. This tool will allow managers to assess their current security situations and continue to enhance security at their particular facility. The ViSAT modules are designed to incorporate industry safety and security best practices for critical infrastructure to assist in establishing a security baseline for each facility. To do so, the ViSAT evaluates current security programs in seven broad categories:

- Security Plans, Policies, and Procedures
- Security Technology Equipment
- Security Force and Security Awareness
- Communication Security Training
- Information Security
- Cargo, Personnel, and Vehicle Access Control
- Physical Security Assets.

Based on the specific information provided by the facility itself, the ViSAT identifies the strengths of current security programs as well as areas in need of improvement, facilitating the prioritization of necessary enhancements to the facility's security. A comprehensive report of the self-assessment can be printed or updated at any time, detailing the effectiveness of the facility's current security plan and providing best practices for implementing future improvements to security programs.

Cyber Vulnerability

One of the potential threats to the security of future special events may be cyber attacks. The National Infrastructure Advisory Council has noted that cyber vulnerability may lead to "an implicit or explicit failure of the confidentiality, integrity, or availability of an information system."[19] The fear is that a group could disrupt a major special event by infiltrating or hacking into on-site information systems that control communications, utilities (electricity, water, heating, cooling), automated locking mechanisms, elevators, or other essential information technology.

The U.S. Secret Service has been leading the effort to develop cyber vulnerability assessments for major special events. The Secret Service has developed a partnership with the Carnegie Mellon

University Software Engineering Institute's CERT® Coordination Center (CERT/CC).[20] The Center is developing protocols to evaluate information technology security risks and implement protective measures. This technology is evolving.

[18] Contact DHS-ViSAT@dhs.gov for more information.

[19] See, National Infrastructure Advisory Council's *Vulnerability Disclosure Framework*, www.dhs.gov/interweb/assetlibrary/vdwgreport.pdf and *The National Strategy to Secure Cyberspace*, White House Report, Office of the President, Washington, D.C., www.whitehouse.gov/pcipb.

[20] See www.cert.org.

Business Impact Analysis

In some major special events, security measures include erecting fencing and Jersey barriers that result in blocking off vehicles and pedestrians from businesses around the special event venue. As a consequence, some businesses may actually experience fewer customers during a major special event. It is incumbent on law enforcement, in planning for special event security measures, to determine the impact of security measures on local businesses.

For example, in downtown Chicago, during the June 2004 Academy of Achievement Summit, the city and U.S. Secret Service erected fencing adjacent to the Peninsula Hotel, where many of the foreign heads of state were housed. This fencing blocked pedestrians from the usual entrances to a number of retail stores. While these security measures affected the businesses, officials from the Chicago Police Department and Secret Service met with business representatives and explained the necessity for the security measures and the limited duration.

For police agencies practicing community policing strategies, meeting with businesses to explain law enforcement programs and obtaining input from the corporate community are common communication techniques in maintaining partnerships.

While in some events, law enforcement security measures impact business operations; in other events, the business community needs law enforcement to provide event security to help the event and private sector make a profit. For example, the downtown Speed Street Festival in Charlotte, North Carolina, has been held for the past ten years. The event holder is the Coca Cola 600 Foundation, which works under a contract with NASCAR. The Foundation's sole purpose is to plan and stage this event, which attracts 100,000 to 120,000 people daily, many of whom are from out of town and out of state. In this case, part of the Charlotte-Mecklenburg Police Department's mission is to help the Foundation (and the city) have an economically successful event.

Discussion of Major Special Event Security Key Functional Areas

1. Determining and Acquiring the Security Workforce

Key Questions to Ask:

- Do we have enough personnel in-house?
- Who should we partner with for additional security forces?
- Who should we partner with for additional authority, skills, equipment, or technology support?
- Do we have officers with Federal Security Clearances?

In most of the major special events reviewed for this guidelines report, the security workforce involved a variety of local law enforcement agencies (lead agency supplemented by other surrounding agencies), fire/EMS agencies, state agencies, private security, and volunteers. Other city, county, or state agencies, such as transportation/traffic, utilities, health, sanitation, and others often supplemented these security personnel. And, depending on the national importance of the event, federal law enforcement agencies were involved.

The first issue addressed by all agencies in the initial security planning stages for a major special event is the need for personnel resources. Planning groups need to think about personnel resource needs in different ways as shown on the next page.

In estimating the number of security personnel needed for a special event, it is always best to err on the side of having too many rather than not having enough. Chief Charles Ramsey, Washington, D.C., Metropolitan Police Department, who has successfully managed security at many special events, including several World Trade Organization meetings with disruptive protestors, contends that having a large "show of force" helps act as a deterrent to disruptive behavior.

Issues to consider in determining and acquiring the security workforce:

- Can we identify all the security assignments/posts that require staffing (inner, middle, and outer perimeter; all transit routes including roads, waterways, air, and more)?

- How many personnel will be needed at each assignment/post?

- How many supervisors will be needed to oversee the personnel at each assignment/post?

- How long will shifts last (8 hours, 12 hours)?

- How much relief will be needed?

- Are we paying overtime to our own officers?

- Are we paying overtime to officers from outside agencies?

- What different types of skills do we need (e.g., information technology specialists, administrative support, dispatchers, canine handlers, bike patrol, horse mounted, etc.)?

- What different types of authority do we need (e.g., prosecutors, civil attorneys, etc.)?

- Will officers need security clearances if they plan to receive federal intelligence information?

Two recent examples of being adequately prepared at special events with enough security forces are illustrative. In the 9th inning of the final game in the 2004 American League Championship Series between the Boston Red Sox and the New York Yankees, fans become angry at an umpire's call that was a turning point in the game. Spectators began throwing objects on the field of play. Within minutes, after being requested by team and league officials, the New York City Police Department was able to summon about 40 standby officers, wearing riot helmets and carrying batons, who came onto the field through the players' dugouts to line up along the right and left field lines—showing that their forces separated the spectators from the field. The forces remained for half an inning of play, then departed when calm was restored.

In contrast, in Auburn Hills, Michigan, on November 19, 2004, toward the end of the National Basketball Association game between the Detroit Pistons and the visiting Indiana Pacers, two players from each team got into a shoving match on the floor after a foul call. As the players were being separated to avoid fighting, some fans close to the Indiana team's bench began throwing objects at the Indiana players. Several Indiana players charged into the crowd and starting fighting with spectators. In a matter of seconds, dozens of players were fighting with dozens of fans. It took security forces about two minutes to pull the players from the stands and restore calm. The game was immediately cancelled. As the Indiana players were being hustled off the floor through the exit to the locker room, additional spectators pelted them with beer, cups, ice, and popcorn. Detroit Pistons coach Larry Brown was quoted as saying, "It's the ugliest thing I've ever seen as a coach or player."[21]

[21]Study team staff observed both situations live on network television broadcasts. See also *The Washington Post*, page D-1, November 20, 2004. It may not be fair to compare the two events. It would be logical that a much larger security force would be available at a League Championship event in contrast to a regular NBA game.

After the number of personnel needed for security is estimated, planning groups can begin to determine how the resources will be acquired. In this stage, the lead agency needs to identify all the other necessary agencies and groups to partner with to effectively secure the event. Thinking about partnering with surrounding law enforcement and federal law enforcement agencies is a natural first step. Below, we discuss some other potential partners—private security, hotel security, and volunteers. We also discuss some specialty support services—canine, mounted patrol, bicycle unit, gang unit, and others.

One area that is often underestimated is the need for adequate staffing for relief. The Philadelphia Welcome America Ceremonies followed by the Greek Picnic put a heavy burden on the Philadelphia Police Department during a two-week period. Scheduling sufficient personnel is difficult and expensive. Officers, supervisors, and commanders can become exhausted without careful attention to good scheduling and sufficient relief forces.

In terms of managing the workforce, the nature of the event may dictate the need for close supervision. More supervisors are needed if an event will draw protestors with intentions to disrupt the event. In these situations, for purposes of monitoring and accountability, a greater number of supervisors and commanders are needed in the field.

As noted earlier, agencies also have to plan for turnover. When key contacts in partner agencies are identified, the lead agency should ask for back-ups. In one event reviewed, a deputy chief from a surrounding agency with a key role in event security retired two weeks before the event. The lead agency had to scramble to fill his role.

Private Sector Security

The private sector owns the organizations, and often the facilities, involved in many of the major national sporting events, concerts, and other public entertainment in the United States. In many of these events, the owners have hired their own private security to work with law enforcement to provide security for the event. Depending on the event, private security may take the lead role in securing the event or take a supporting role to law enforcement. However, in some private special events, law enforcement may not be involved at all.

These guidelines are helpful in those situations where the private event management company involves local law enforcement in the planning and implementation of security for the event. There are many privately managed events, especially concerts, in which the private management company also manages the entire security. Public law enforcement may not be involved at all in these events, unless called to the scene to handle disturbances or crimes.

For these types of private events, especially in smaller venues, the local city and county governments should take a closer look at security planning and implementation and consider policies or legislation to require more cooperation between the private event managers and law enforcement. In a 2002 survey of 31 rock and rap concerts worldwide (11 in the U.S.), the Crowd Management Strategies organization found that there were 20 deaths and over 4,000 injuries—in just 31 out of hundreds of concerts. The organization also notes in its survey report that even after 9/11, the U.S. concert industry shows "no consistent security improvements to counter possible terrorist attacks…" and that "the most vulnerable events will be those that use festival/standing room environments, fail to take prudent security and crowd safety steps, fail to adequately train private security and have no emergency plans."[22]

[22] See *Crowd Management Strategies*, Eleventh Rock Concert Safety Survey, at www.crowdsafe.com.

On December 8, 2004, in Columbus, Ohio, a disillusioned fan of a rock band jumped a security fence, climbed on stage, and shot and killed four members of the band and spectators. Police officers patrolling nearby responded to the scene and killed the assailant. Reportedly, concert security guards were present at the event.[23]

In an example of limited responsibility, at the Salt Lake City Olympics, Wackenhut Corporation assisted with security access at some venues, screening transport vehicles that moved spectators from parking lots to venues. In a shared responsibility example, for many of the National Football League games and college sporting events, the force of private security staff equals (or sometimes outnumbers) law enforcement. The NFL headquarters also has its own security force that provides assistance and monitors the security at league games.

In contrast, for some sporting events, such as professional tennis, Professional Golf Association events, and concerts, the inner perimeter security is made up mostly of private security. Law enforcement generally only provides traffic and outside area support. Local law enforcement coordinates with many different types of organizations that employ security personnel or contract with private security firms—not just hotels, stadiums, arenas, and concert halls, but also carnival companies, churches, theme parks, shopping malls, museums, corporate foundations, and non-profit organizations.

Regardless of the exact nature of the working relationship between law enforcement and private security, when it comes to security of major special events, law enforcement must be prepared to partner with private security.[24] Private security has a vital role to play in planning and managing the security of major special events.

For some events, law enforcement might even consider contracting with private security personnel to help supplement law enforcement's security responsibilities, if the need arises. Additionally, some of the larger national and international private security firms have experts who are experienced in planning security for major special events.

Hotel Security

One of the more critical relationships for law enforcement to cultivate is with hotel security. Spectators attending every major special event stay in hotels. The hotel security staff can act as a "force multiplier" for security at special events. For major special events, law enforcement should have a contact list (cell phones, pagers) for hotel security directors. For hotels close to the event and hotels where many of the event spectators are staying, law enforcement should conduct a "walk through" of the hotels and personally coordinate with hotel security. In some cases, if law enforcement has the capacity and technology, they should enter hotel floor plans into communications command center computers. Law enforcement should also make sure that the hotel has been recently inspected by the fire marshal's office to see that alarms and security technology are in working order.

In some cases, the hotel is the special event venue. The Oscar De La Hoya vs. Shane Mosley world championship boxing match, held at the MGM Grand Hotel in September 2003, presented several challenges to the Las Vegas Metro Police Department (LVMPD). The hotel received permission from the fire department to increase seating to 18,500, over the arena's normal capacity of 13,500; there was an "adversarial atmosphere" with overzealous fans, many of whom had been drinking; and there was a contentious relationship between fighters and fight camps. Over 100 LVMPD personnel were assigned to this event.

[23] The band, Damageplan, was playing at the Alrosa Villa. More information can be found at www.mtv.com.

[24] See IACP/COPS *National Policy Summit: Building Private Security/Public Policing Partnerships to Prevent and Respond to Terrorism and Public Disorder* at www.cops.usdoj.gov/mime/open.pdf?item=1355.

On the night before the fight, officers were assigned to the weigh-in area, casino area (to look for ticket scalpers), and box office. On fight night, a uniformed LVMPD officer was stationed at each of the ring corners. Officers also assisted with fighter escort for the main bouts, were assigned to the dressing room areas, and were stationed at all ticket turnstiles and in the concourse areas. The idea was to be sure patrons knew that police were present ("Nobody gets in without seeing a police officer"). Traffic officers were also assigned outside the arena. LVMPD credited the number of pre-event meetings held with hotel security and the detail involved in those meetings as "the lynchpin for the overall success of the event." Hotel security representatives belong to the Security Chiefs Association in Las Vegas, which was described as "very in tune" to providing training on post-9/11 security threats.

Volunteers

Volunteers are used to supplement security in many special events. One example of law enforcement working with volunteers to provide security at special events includes the Christopher Street West Association's (a non-profit service organization within the gay and lesbian community of greater Los Angeles) annual parade and celebration hosted by the city of West Hollywood. The organization provides about 1,000 volunteers to assist law enforcement with security. The Los Angeles County Sheriff's Department, which secures the parade route, attributes much of the event's success to excellent cooperation and planning with Christopher Street West. Security planning for the Tournament of Roses Parade/Rose Bowl Game includes year-round coordination with the Tournament of Roses Association. This is a non-profit organization dedicated to producing these events. It has a staff of 35 and approximately 1,200 volunteers that help with security.

On the plus side, using volunteers to supplement security forces provides low-cost personnel resources and, in some situations, shows police-community collaboration. The limitations are that volunteers have restricted usage—often assisting with access control on the outer perimeter—and may feel neglected because they are so far away from the event. In the Salt Lake City Olympics, the research group found that many volunteers working out in the cold at remote access points felt that they were not given enough recognition. (Greene, 2002).

If the volunteers remain in the outer perimeter, their credentialing involves minimal work. However, if volunteers are permitted to work the middle or inner perimeter, then more work is required to conduct background checks on them. This is discussed more under the section on credentialing.

Police agencies practicing community policing strategies have often already developed partnerships with private security and hotel security and often use volunteers for many police programs.[25]

Specialty Security Services

The lead event security agency needs to determine the variety of specialty resources that might provide support to secure major special events. Of course, the need for these resources must be weighed against their availability (if not available in the lead agency, identify which agency can assist) and cost. Some examples of specialty services commonly deployed at special events are mentioned below.

Explosive Detection Canines and Handlers. For major special events, canines trained to detect improvised explosive devices (IEDs) are used extensively to sweep protected areas. Some of the best-trained and experienced explosive detection canines are part of the Department of Defense and the Bureau of Alcohol, Tobacco, Firearms, and Explosives. Dogs and handlers from these agencies are sometimes used for national special events supported by federal law enforcement. All ATF special agent canine handlers are certified explosive specialists. ATF's protocols for security sweeps and issues related to package assessments might also be helpful to state and local bomb squads.

Generally, the perceived value of explosive detection canines depends on the extent to which an area can be physically and permanently secured after a sweep. Working explosive detection canines can also become fatigued. The number of dogs needed should be considered when deciding whether to sweep large venues.

In our review of special events managed by local law enforcement, explosive detection canines were not used routinely for every large local or regional event, although it was common to conduct explosives sweeps of stadiums and arenas (e.g., the Rose Bowl, some college football games, political events) and concert halls (sometimes routinely, and sometimes depending on the particular performers). For example, for private events in Las Vegas hotels (sporting exhibitions, concerts, conventions), the Las Vegas Metro Police conduct dog sweeps when a specific threat has been identified but not as a matter of routine.

Law enforcement also shares canine resources. For example, in Columbus, Ohio, providing public safety at Ohio State University (OSU) football games (110,000 people) involves four police agencies: the Columbus Police Department, Franklin County Sheriff's Department, State Highway Patrol, and OSU police. The stadium is swept by dogs from the Franklin County Sheriff's Department and State Highway Patrol. This process begins at 4:00 a.m. before every game. IED sweeps are also done at other events. For example, for the Columbus Marathon (7,000 runners), the formation area, newspaper boxes, and other areas are swept; and for the Red White and Blue festival, the Columbus Fire Department bomb unit sweeps all vendors and unattended coolers. The extent to which Columbus law enforcement agencies make use of explosive detection canines for sweeps, however, may be beyond many other agencies' capabilities and resources.

Mounted Units. Police departments with mounted units (Denver, Portland, Austin, Indianapolis, and others) consistently praised the advantages of horses as a "force multiplier." As one tactical operations commander explained, "Four or five horses can clear out a crowd that might take a whole platoon of officers on foot to disburse." Another noted their popularity with spectators as well as their benefits for crowd control.

One drawback is the possibility that the horses will "get spooked," which happened some years ago in Portland. Since then, Portland has not deployed horses for special events on a routine basis, although they have proved valuable stationed in twos or threes for events like the Fat Tuesday street celebration held in the city's entertainment district. The department has also found that on more clearly problematic, potentially violent protests they are very useful. However, on more mainstream, peaceful protests, their presence can be counter-productive since they tend to draw an adverse crowd reaction— they can signal crowd dispersal on permitted events when that is not the message the police and city want to send.

The other obvious drawback to mounted units is cost. Several departments expressed regret that their mounted units—despite the advantages they provide for crowd control—have been cut back because of reductions in budgets.

Bicycle Units. Several departments discussed the benefits of deploying bicycle officers at special events. The key advantages involve quicker and better access and use in crowd control.

In terms of access, at a variety of special events, law enforcement has used officers on bicycles to quickly maneuver through vehicle traffic and crowded areas to reach incidents where officers were needed. For the 2004 Republican National Convention, the NYPD trained over 300 officers and equipped them with bicycles to serve as a mobile field force during the event. In fact, the use of the bikes proved so popular that some of the police legal advisors, who were in the field to observe and offer on the spot legal advice to supervisors, also rode bikes to get through the crowds quickly.

The bicycles have also been used for crowd control during events with protestors and demonstrations. Police agencies in Washington, D.C., Philadelphia, and Indianapolis have used bike officers to form a temporary barrier and found the "portable fence" to be effective in various crowd control situations.

Motorcycle Units. Motorcycles have been used successfully for years by some police agencies as part of their overall crowd control tactics. They run up and down streets at the curb lane to keep crowd members on the sidewalk and out of the street or other designated areas.

Gang Units. Several departments discussed deploying gang units at special events known to attract gang members and associates. One department mentioned that its gang officers had briefed and worked closely with state troopers who were assisting at an event (previously, the troopers had little occasion to become familiar with the jurisdiction's gang-related concerns).

Other Specialized Units. Drug and vice officers were assigned to work undercover at a number of local and regional events. At some events, undercover officers enforced alcohol laws (sales to minors). Fraud detectives may also be assigned to some events (e.g., to identify ticket scalpers). A post-blast investigation team may also be deployed in events that have experienced explosions. If the event includes water access (e.g., riverfront stadium), security support may need to include water patrol (at the federal level, agencies receive support from the U.S. Coast Guard and dive teams).

2. Communications and Communication Technology

Inter-Agency Communication

Key Questions to Ask:

Do we have a process in place to communicate regularly with all key partners?

Do we have adequate communications technology and equipment?

Do we have adequate communications back up?

Can we integrate radio communication among many different agencies involved in the event?

Are communications command center facilities adequate in size and scope?

[26] Flynn, Dan. *After Action Report , G-8 Summit—Savannah/ Sea Island, Georgia*, Savannah-Chatham Police Department, September 15, 2004.

Over 75 years ago, the poet W.B. Yeats noted that man should "think like a wise man but communicate in the language of the people." Savannah-Chatham Police Chief Dan Flynn recounts that when he was preparing security for the 2004 G-8 Summit in Sea Island, Georgia, the city was visited by the Mayor of Calgary, which had hosted the June 2003 World Trade Organization Summit.

The Mayor indicated that the security forces in Calgary and Canada were concerned because of the violence that had occurred at WTO events in Seattle and Genoa. Calgary handled the event smoothly and without any major problems in large part because of a well-crafted and implemented communication plan that was supported and stressed by all key security partners. Chief Flynn notes, in his department's After Action Report on the G-8 Summit:

> …the Calgary officials most attributed their success to the quality of their communication plan. That plan focused heavily on perfecting their communications and dialogue internally with all staff and partner government agencies, externally with the general public, and perhaps most importantly with the leaders and members of identifiable protest groups.[26]

Thus, one very important principle in security planning for major special events is to create policies and procedures for all partners, governing officials, private security, and others to communicate regularly on event planning and management. All parties should use e-mail, with its distribution list and storage capabilities, extensively to keep all partners up-to-date and informed on plans, decisions, agreements, issues, and more.

For larger events, the lead agency could develop a special secure web site that could include a variety of materials such as venue floor plans, hotel floor plans, city/county maps, aerial photos, etc. However, there is a risk that such a web site, even though secured and protected with the latest technology, could be hacked. Thus, highly sensitive and confidential plans should not be on such a site.

Radio Communication Interoperability

As noted in earlier examples, security for most major special events includes personnel from many different agencies—including law enforcement, fire, EMS, transportation, and others; and from city, county, state, and federal levels. These personnel come to the event with radios that are different models and with different frequencies. The goal is to have all field personnel be able to communicate with each other at the event in order to coordinate security.

For some special events, depending on the size of the security force, the lead agency may be able to disseminate radios on the same frequencies to all security personnel. In some past Super Bowl events, vendors have loaned radios to the lead agency to distribute to the field. In the Washington, DC, region, the Council of Governments (COG) has purchased over 400 radios that are stored in a warehouse for use by law enforcement at special events and emergency situations.

More commonly for radio interoperability in today's major special events, where officers and others from many different agencies assist at the event using their own radios, the lead agency relies on advanced communications technology to link radios with different frequencies[27] into a common communications matrix. This evolving technology acts as a networking gateway that interconnects radios with any frequencies into a common event frequency.[28] The effectiveness of this technology and approach has been demonstrated at many major special events including the dedication ceremonies for the World War II monument, the President's Inauguration, and other special events. At the August 2003 Professional Golf Association (PGA) championship, the Monroe County, New York, Sheriff's Office (Rochester area) reports that it tested the technology to connect radio frequencies together. In future events, they plan to interconnect radio communications among private security. Some tips for radio communications protocol at special events are shown below.

In some of the special events observed by the study team, even normal radio communication was at times excessive and often inaudible. During a real emergency, radio communication might become so overwhelming as to be confusing and dangerous.

A key decision for the lead agency is assigning radio channels and radio access to multiple agencies in support roles at special events. Some of the options include the following:

1. Assign radios only to team supervisors (e.g., a sergeant overseeing 8-10 officers) at key posts. The supervisor can communicate any news to the officers. This keeps officer access to a minimum. However, if officers ever get separated from the team, they will be without radios.

2. Assign radios to all officers but enable the radios with "monitor only" access on the main channel. Officers can transmit on another channel, keeping the main channel with limited access.

3. Assign a variety of channels for different functions and purposes, thus not overloading any one channel. This requires more dispatchers to monitor the channels.

The current interoperable communications technology is evolving to include wireless transmission of voice and data.[29] However, one of the lessons learned from the G-8 Summit in Georgia is that despite multiple means of sophisticated communications, many officers still relied on their own cell phones.

[27] Public safety agencies use a variety of radio frequency spectrum in the U.S. including VHF (150-174 MHz), UHF (450-512 MHz), 800 MHz, etc.

[28] For more information on these radio interoperability communication networks, see DHS' SAFECOM Program Office (www.safecomprogram.gov). See also, the National Institute of Justice's CommTech program, formerly the AGILE program at www.agileprogram.org, which includes a useful report located at www.agileprogram.org/documents/TE-02-03.pdf. See also, the Public Safety Wireless Network, www.pswn.org.

[29] See the Capital Wireless Integrated Network (CapWIN) at www.capwinproject.com; see also, Mulholland, David, "Interagency Communications During Major Events Possible," *The Police Chief*, International Association of Chiefs of Police, July 2004, p. 17 and www.safecomprogram.gov.

Tips for Radio Communications Protocol at Special Events

- Lead agency should send a survey form to all assisting agencies requesting information on radios—models, frequencies, contact for technical problems, etc.

- Check ('ping') all radios in the field the day of the event before activities begin to ensure all radios are operational and personnel are on the proper frequencies.

- Don't use '10 codes' on the radio—different agencies working the event have different definitions.

- Create and disseminate clear and consistent radio identification codes for all assignments. For example, use the agency name first (when multiple agencies are assisting), then a call number, e.g., 'Alexandria 15.'

- Ensure that radio chargers are available in key locations in the field.

- Brief personnel and distribute handouts on radio channels to use (e.g., channel 1 for outer perimeter, channel 2 for inner perimeter, channel 3 for emergencies, etc.) and protocols (limit chatter, assume anyone with a scanner can pick up your transmission, etc.).

- Establish check-in system to ensure that all outside agencies bring in radios to lead agency to enter frequencies into communications network, if the technology is available. This allows lead agency to check quality of radios—as Alexandria (Virginia) Police Department Captain Eddie Reyes, the AGILE project director, points out, 'Radios have to be operable before they can be interoperable.'

An issue that comes up in planning security at major special events is the need to use encryption technology for radio transmissions to protect from outsiders intercepting transmissions. At present, it is more difficult to program encrypted radios into network gateways. Thus, the role of radio encryption at major special events is still evolving.

In addition, the use of other mobile computing communication devices, such as personal data assistants (PDAs), handheld computers, smart phones, and the like will rapidly change the nature of field communications at major special events.[30]

Integrated Communications Command Center

One of the most important components in planning security for major special events is to develop an integrated communications command center. The integrated communications command center brings together key leaders and actors from all the agencies and jurisdictions involved in supporting security at the event.

At the federal level, examples of integrated communications command centers include the DHS Joint Field Office (JFO); DHS/U.S. Secret Service's Multi-Agency Command Center (MACC); the Bomb Management Center (BMC); and the FBI's Joint Operations Center (JOC).

[30] See article on Massachusetts State Police using wireless devices at Logan Airport to perform background checks on suspicious persons, www.pcworld.com/news.

On-scene coordination is most often managed in accordance with the principles of the Incident Command System (ICS), a component of the National Incident Management System (NIMS). Principles of ICS can also be applied to the operation of integrated communications command centers. The DHS NIMS Integration Center (NIC) establishes standards and training related to NIMS and ICS, and training is available through the Federal Emergency Management Agency (FEMA). NIMS is a comprehensive incident response system, developed by the Department of Homeland Security at the request of the President (Homeland Security Presidential Directive/HSPD-5). The Integration Center is in the process of developing standards, guidelines, protocols, and more to support incident management response development at the state and local level. One of the main tools being supported with training and technical assistance is the ICS approach.[31] A paper on NIMS and the Incident Command System[32] notes the following:

> The NIMS represents a core set of doctrines, principles, terminology, and organizational processes to enable effective, efficient and collaborative incident management at all levels. To provide the framework for interoperability and compatibility, the NIMS is based on a balance between flexibility and standardization. The recommendations of the National Commission on Terrorist Attacks Upon the United States (the "9/11 Commission") further highlight the importance of ICS (incident command system). The Commission's recent report recommends national adoption of the ICS to enhance command, control and communications capabilities.

The NIMS Integration Center and FEMA provide training for state and local public safety agencies on ICS.[33] The following ICS management characteristics, among others, are taught by DHS in its ICS training programs:

- Common Terminology
- Reliance on an Incident Action Plan
- Manageable Span of Control
- Pre-designated Incident Mobilization Center Locations & Facilities
- Integrated Communications
- Chain of Command and Unity of Command
- Information and Intelligence Management
- Unified Command.

The paper on NIMS and the Incident Command System describes unified command as follows:

> Unified Command (UC) is an important element in multi-jurisdictional or multi-agency domestic incident management. It provides guidelines to enable agencies with different legal, geographic, and functional responsibilities to coordinate, plan, and interact effectively. As a team, the Unified Command overcomes much of the inefficiency and duplication of effort that can occur when agencies from different functional and geographic jurisdictions, or agencies at different levels of government, operate without a common system or organizational framework. The primary difference between the single command structure and the UC structure is that in a single command structure, the IC (incident commander) is solely responsible for establishing incident management objectives and strategies. In a UC structure, the individuals designated by their jurisdictional authorities jointly determine objectives, plans, and priorities and work together to execute them.

[31] See www.usfa.fema.gov/downloads/pdf/tr_00dc.pdf.

[32] See the NIMS web site at www.fema.gov/nims.

[33] See Herron, Shawn, "The National Incident Management System," The Police Chief, November 2004, p. 20-25.

Some common features of a centralized communications command center using an ICS approach for security of major special events include the following:

- Facility should be adequate to house key leaders and representatives from each agency involved in supporting security at the event. There were over 50 agency representatives in the USSS MACC at the Boston Democratic National Convention, including law enforcement (local, state, federal), prosecutors (county, U.S. Attorney's Office), Coast Guard, National Guard, transit authority, medical agencies, and others.

- Ideally, rows of seating should be tiered like a movie theater to improve visibility. At the Democratic National Convention, the USSS used a U.S. Department of Transportation auditorium for the MACC. They hired a company to pull out the theater seats and put in tiered platforms.

- Agency names should be visible on name tents—helps to readily identify key representatives.

- Ideally, the room should have a raised stage up front for easily visible briefings.

- Room should have good lighting, adequate voice amplification sound system, readily accessible bathrooms and a break room with beverages.

- Facility should contain private conference rooms for special meetings, if available.

- Access to the facility should be secured with adequate screening.

- Facility should have high speed Internet access for e-mail, data transfer, database management, and more.

- All laptops from each agency should be networked together. Outside agency laptops need to be screened for viruses before being allowed to connect to the network.

- Facility should have a "video wall" that shows live video feeds of event venues, traffic and street activities, local and national news, and video from air support, if possible. Use of security cameras will be discussed more in the next section.

- Videoconferencing technology is useful, if available.

- Equipment and technology vendors should be on site, as well as agency computer technicians that set up the facility.

- Contact information (name, phone #, cell phone #, pager #, radio call #, etc.) for all key persons should be downloaded on each laptop and conspicuously posted on a chart in the room.

The U.S. Secret Service's Multi-Agency Command Center (MACC) is one of the best implementation models for developing an integrated communications command center to help monitor and manage security at major special events. The study team observed several highly advanced joint operations communications command centers during this project, including the USSS' MACC used for the 2004 Democratic National Convention, the New York City Police Department's communications command center used for the 2004 Republican National Convention, and the Washington, D.C., Metropolitan Police Department's communications command center used for the World War II memorial commemoration, President Reagan's funeral procession in D.C., and several WTO events.

The central features of integrated communications command centers, like the MACCs, are the multiple video viewing screens that may portray dozens of different video feeds simultaneously, and the management system. The centers use a centralized incident management system. The incident commander, or designee, screens all incident notifications that can be forwarded via e-mail by anyone in the room. These "incidents" need to be screened to avoid overwhelming the posted event incident screen with nuisance calls ("a spectator's vehicle backed into the bumper of one of the EMS vehicles in the North parking lot")—only the most important incidents (e.g., suspicious packages, arrests, protestor movements, etc.) should be posted on the event incident monitoring screen to provide an ongoing log for all persons in the facility to view. The incident management system shows current incidents, time, location, and whether they were resolved ("suspicious backpack reported abandoned at corner of 10th & Court Street at 1:15 pm—EOD responded—school books found inside—pack removed from scene"). The commander also makes the call for the proper field unit to investigate or handle the incident and then logs the resolution. It is also important to communicate to key commanders and supervisors in the field that suspected threats have been addressed and resolved.

The incident management system also contains the capability for users to review the history of event incidents for the day. This can be done on individual laptops. In some MACCs, standalone computers are placed along the sides of the room with screens set on event histories.

In a federally managed event, the MACC commander coordinates with the FBI JOC and/or Intelligence Operations Center to determine the proper field unit to investigate or handle field incidents.

In developing an integrated communications command center for a special event, the center should be able to access and observe the routine calls for service that are being dispatched on the local law enforcement's computer-assisted dispatch (CAD) system. A CAD terminal should be located, along with an experienced dispatcher, in the command center. The command center should know about routine police calls that are occurring throughout the city or county that could possibly have some relationship to event security.

The FBI has developed a virtual private network system that allows secure remote access to the incident monitoring system. This Virtual Command Center (VCC) is administered through the FBI's Law Enforcement Online (LEO) program. The LEO VCC has been used for all NSSEs and several non-NSSEs since the 2004 Democratic National Convention in Boston. The USSS is developing a similar system for future use at major special events. This will enable USSS headquarters personnel or the local city Mayor's staff, for example, to view and monitor event incidents live via secure Internet access. Intelligence briefings are delivered periodically throughout the day and night at the integrated communications command center. At the Democratic National Convention, the FBI from the Boston Joint Terrorism Task Force (JTTF) would often conduct the briefings. In order for people in the center to know when the briefings would occur, the briefings schedule for the day was posted on a flip chart at the front of the room.

One of the most critical parts of the communications plan is to have a contingency plan—a back-up communications capability that is located away from the event venue in case the central communications command center is destroyed or incapable of operating. The back-up should function from a generator in case access to electricity is a problem. Many agencies have mobile communications vans that can serve as the back-up. The van should also have satellite telephone access in case all local systems, including wireless, are overloaded.

It is also important to have access to data and information (resources, GIS maps, etc.). This information should be backed up and stored at an off-site location.

Delivering training to all communications center participants is also very useful. Once all event security partners are assembled in the communications center, the lead agency should facilitate a tabletop exercise that involves handling a variety of possible scenarios. The guidelines will discuss more on training in Section 13.

3. Access Control: Screening and Physical Security

Access Planning and Management

> **Key Questions to Ask:**
>
> Do we have clearly specified perimeters: inner, middle, outer?
>
> Do we have adequate and appropriate security for each perimeter?
>
> Do we have enough technical equipment for effective and efficient screening?
>
> Do we have enough staff for timely screening?
>
> Do we have staff trained and experienced in screening?
>
> Do we have proper screening protocols?
>
> Are screening regulations clearly posted for all participants to read?

Access control is critical in securing major special events. It is important to be able to differentiate among spectators or fans that have paid or have tickets to enter an event and performers, VIPs, officials, and others who have the privilege or permission to be "backstage" at the event. The credentialing process is discussed in Section 6.

Security professionals recommend planning access control in terms of three perimeters—outer, middle, and inner. Security concerns and issues related to each perimeter will be presented below. Exhibit 3 illustrates a simplistic schematic showing the three security perimeters.

Outer Perimeter Security

The outer perimeter is often referred to as the "first line of defense." The National Football League's Best Practices for Stadium Security refer to securing the outer perimeter as follows:

> Establish a 100-foot secure outer perimeter around the stadium to the maximum extent possible. Protect areas vulnerable to forced vehicle entry with substantial barricades. Include the use of Jersey barriers, reinforced concrete decorative planters, bollards and/or large trucks or buses. Configure the barriers in such a manner as to prevent any type of forced vehicle entry. Close roads and streets adjacent to the facility, where feasible.

Outer perimeter security is used to deter vehicle traffic but not necessarily pedestrian traffic. One key security concern is vehicle bombs. Depending on the scale and importance of the event, security forces may also place counter-surveillance teams, mobile field forces, and fixed posts in and around the outer perimeter.

Middle Perimeter Security

The middle perimeter is the first level of access control for persons and their possessions. This perimeter is secured so that no one without a pass/ticket or credential is permitted entry through protected gates or doors. Depending on the scale and importance of the special event, screening participants at this level may involve a combination of the following, ranging from less to more security:

Persons:

- (a) visual inspection, (b) require person to open outer clothing, (c) pat down outer clothing, (d) use magnetometer wands to scan clothing, (e) place all jackets and outer clothing through an x-ray machine.

- Post uniformed officer at each gate to observe suspicious behavior and to back up screeners.

Possessions/Objects:

- Prohibit any large objects—coolers, backpacks, large bags, etc. (that could be used to conceal explosives or weapons).

- Visual inspection and search of all handbags, binocular cases, briefcases, etc.

- Use magnetometers to scan all handbags, binocular cases, briefcases, etc.

It is always advisable to publicize and clearly post the policy related to inspections and to identify prohibited items. The NFL's Best Practices for Stadium Security states that team owners should:

- Publicize the policy concerning inspections and identify prohibited items.

- Send notices to season ticket holders.

- Post signage and distribute leaflets at the stadiums, satellite parking areas, and logical transit sites.

- Use loop announcements and staff at key locations to provide information concerning allowable/prohibited items.

For the 2004 Kentucky Derby Race, the following list of prohibited items was highly publicized and posted in parking lots and access gates at Churchill Downs:

- Weapons of any kind, including knives and scissors

- Alcohol of any type

- Bottles/cans of any kind, including beverage/lotion containers made of glass, plastic, or metal

- Thermoses

- Coolers

- Grills

- Backpacks, luggage, and duffel bags

- Wagons

- Umbrellas.

Exhibit 3. Perimeter Security Planning Illustration

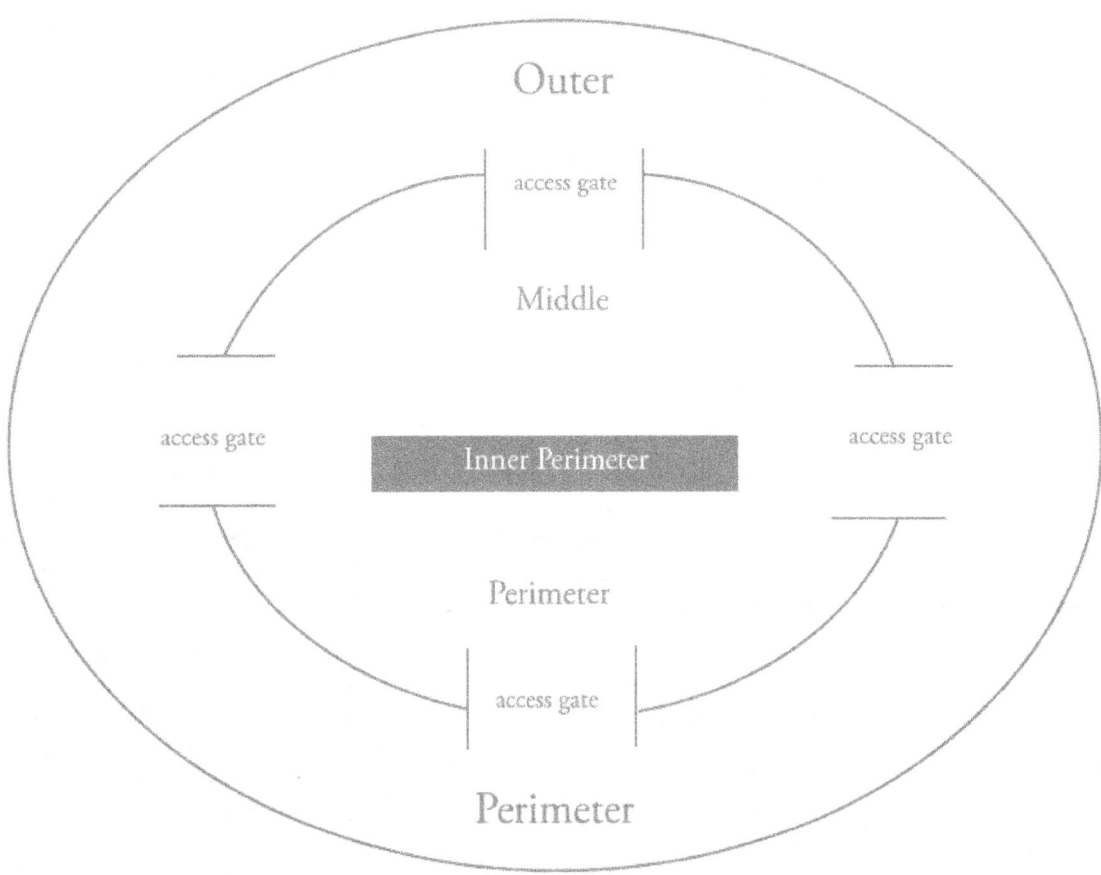

For major sporting and other special events, the media might also be helpful in publicizing what items will be allowed into the event.

Pasadena police report that securing the Rose Bowl stadium generally follows NFL best practices recommendations. The stadium private security firm, which contracts with the Tournament of Roses Association, is also an NFL contractor. A photo identification system is used for everyone working at the stadium. Credentials with ID are checked on all persons entering the stadium and other areas beyond public access, and are cross-referenced against a list maintained by the private security firm; all entering the stadium are subject to searches. There are three levels of searches for various events at the stadium: Level A includes visual inspection of purses at small events (e.g., swap meets); Level B includes inspection of garments, and bags are searched by security personnel, who are supervised by police; and Level C includes full pat-down searches. The Pasadena police are prepared for Level C if a specific threat warrants this. A special events commander notes that this "might require entry six hours early, but the event will take place."

Middle perimeter gate access control must take inspections and screening timing into account. How long will it take to screen participants? The length of time to screen participants will be a factor in setting the time that the gates are open for participants to begin entering the venue. When the gates are opened, security inspections and screening staff must be ready. Long lines and waiting time at access gates may cause participants to become unruly and disorderly. As one security expert put it, "It would be nice if we could tell patrons to 'come early and come naked' so we could run them through screening quickly."

At one special event studied, the plan was to use handheld magnetometers (wands) on all who entered, but the stadium gates were opened only an hour before event time. The planned screening process was too slow and had to be modified on site. In order to have ample space and time for screening, at the 2004 Democratic National Convention, the magnetometers were moved outside to the entry sidewalk so that delegates could walk off their buses and get into a screening line.

Similar security screening must also occur with venue employees; sports team players, coaches, and staff; media; and others. Screening and inspections must be consistent to avoid displaying vulnerabilities in access.

The screeners used at special events are often private security. The lead law enforcement agency needs to make sure these security staff have been trained and follow the inspection protocols. The inspections screening positions and responsibilities should be separate from ticket takers so as to avoid any double duty. Law enforcement are often posted at the access gates to observe suspicious behavior and to back up the screeners.

The NASCAR Minimum Security Standards recommend establishing a "trouble desk" at strategic access points to resolve identification and pass issues. During football games, the University of California/Berkeley stations staff at the student access gate. These staff are equipped with computers and can access student and university files to check whether students have valid identification and have paid for the game, if screeners find a problem.

Law enforcement and event organizers also have to establish a policy on allowing event spectators to leave the venue and reenter again. Some major events, such as NASCAR races, allow it because the entire venue (e.g., exhibit stands) is often spread out beyond the stadium. Security may place wristbands on people leaving the stadium to alert other screeners that this person has been allowed inside already. Many major sporting events (most Division I college football games) don't allow spectators to reenter after they leave the event—they fear people will drink more alcohol or use drugs in the parking lot.

At many venues, participants' parking is beyond the outer perimeter. Security in these locations may involve preventing breaking and entering, auto theft, and vandalism. However, at some venues, middle perimeter security may include parking control. For example, venue staff or VIPs may be allowed to park at a garage under the stadium. In these situations, security decisions must be made and protocols developed regarding (a) level of vehicle inspection (visual, undercarriage viewing, bomb dog sweeps, etc.),[34] (b) tagging vehicles to show other security forces that the vehicle has been inspected and is allowed to park in a restricted area; and

[34] See the Technical Support Working Group's vehicle inspection checklist for detecting improvised explosives at www.tswg.gov/tswg/prods_pubs/VICPress.htm.

(c) towing vehicles that do not comply with rules (even if they belong to security forces). A senior security supervisor who was in charge of a middle perimeter venue surrounding the hotel for many event VIPs noted that one of his best security tools was the tow truck.

Inner Perimeter Security

The Secret Service refers to the inner perimeter as the "last line of defense." Depending on the nature of the event and venue, the inner perimeter contains all the high-level government officials, performers, sports players, VIPs, and their invited guests. The inner perimeter may be the stage and backstage at a theater or political event, the playing field and players' benches in a sporting event, the infield at a horse racing or NASCAR event, and the like. As described in the section on credentialing, people given access to the inner perimeter are screened in advance of the event generally with background checks. No one is ever allowed into the inner perimeter without proper identification and permission.

Establishing inner perimeter security often means setting up additional check and access points where people attempting to enter are screened very carefully. The screening at this stage is for the proper credentials, since the people have already passed through the access gate screening.

One of the key security aspects of inner perimeter security is that some areas are often inspected and swept for explosives and weapons and then secured long before the arrival of the VIPs.

Some law enforcement agencies reported that one group they sometimes have difficulty with on the inner perimeter is personal bodyguards of VIPs and political officials, including foreign dignitaries. Security for the event needs to know who these bodyguards are and to what degree they have been vetted to receive credentials. Are they allowed to remain armed in the inner perimeter? These are issues that need to be resolved by the primary event security agency in advance of the event.

Security Video Cameras

The use of security video cameras has increased at major special events. There were reported to be over 1,600 video cameras used at the 2004 Summer Olympics in Athens.[35] The city of Jacksonville, Florida, contracted with a private firm to build a network of over 100 security cameras to provide video surveillance at Super Bowl XXXIX in February 2005. The cameras monitored key areas of Alltel Stadium and parts of the downtown.

Cameras can double as logistical and security tools. Staff monitors the cameras to detect and record attempted security breaches but also to observe the movements of dignitaries, performers, or speakers to ensure the timing of events. A review of security at the 2004 G-8 Summit in Georgia notes that the organizers "wanted to have the ability to track these events and to know when one event was starting and when another event was ending."[36]

Organizers found it more reassuring to see on video screens the movement of multiple motorcades or multiple helicopters taking off and landing rather than hearing the status on the radio or by phone.

Security personnel can also use video cameras to identify someone who commits a crime (spectator, protestor) and arrest them later when it might cause less of a disruptive scene.[37] Digital video can be stored and searched long after the event.

[35] Walker, Leslie, "High-Tech Security's Olympic Moment," *The Washington Post*, August 12, 2004, page E-1.

[36] Gips, Michael, "An Island of Protection," *Security Management*, September 2004.

[37] After the Tampa Police Department's experience with facial recognition software used during a Super Bowl event, most law enforcement agencies are waiting for this technology to evolve more before using it.

It seems that most large special events venues today are equipped with security video cameras. Some examples include the following:

- In the Best Practices for Stadium Security, the National Football League has urged owners to "install internal and external cameras (digital) with pan, tilt, zoom and monitoring capability covering all vulnerable areas."

- Rose Bowl stadium has eight digital video cameras within the stadium area (parking lot, field, locker rooms, tunnels).

- Charlotte-Mecklenburg police report that having additional video cameras downtown, installed after 9/11, has been one of its biggest assets for managing the Speed Street festival, enabling police to see deeper into the crowd and manage traffic more effectively. Currently, there are 12 video cameras downtown.

- Downtown Phoenix has eight video cameras that monitor and record special events (major sports arenas and concert halls also have video cameras).

- San Diego County Sheriff's Department reports extensive digital video camera surveillance at the San Diego County Fair. Video cameras are operated by the Fairgrounds and monitored at the on-site communications center.

In the future, more video surveillance cameras will operate on broadband wireless networks. However, there are reliability and security issues with transmitting video images over radio spectrum.

Use of security video cameras on the streets may be growing, but public acceptance is not necessarily universal. For example, Portland, Oregon, has not installed video cameras outdoors anywhere in the city. Police suggest it is unlikely that the citizens of Portland would easily accept video cameras on the streets.

In contrast to using video cameras, the Tulsa County (Oklahoma) Sheriff's Office notes limitations on the value of security video cameras for monitoring crowds at the Tulsa State Fair. It reports that setting up 20-foot "deer stands" on the midway for observation has been more useful than video cameras in this venue. A team of deputies protects the base of the stands.

In addition to using video cameras, many law enforcement agencies position officers on rooftops or other high vantage points to observe crowd behavior during special events. For example, in Columbus, Ohio, for the Red White and Blue festival, police use an elevated "scissors jack" hydraulic platform (this is in addition to video cameras with live feeds placed on buildings, officer observations from rooftops, helicopters, and other measures). Two officers go up on the platform and another stays down to guard it. Police report that because the officers can be seen by the crowd, the crowd is much more orderly.

Vendors and Deliveries

Food and beverages are a key part of all special events. Vendors need to make deliveries of these and other goods to special event facilities and venues. However, this is a potentially vulnerable area that requires careful security planning.

During the 2004 Democratic National Convention, the Secret Service and Boston Police Department established elaborate inspection plans for selected and identified companies with vans to deliver food and other supplies to vendors in the Fleet Center. The drivers were screened with background checks. The vans were screened and inspected (including bomb dog sweeps) at an off-site "safe zone"—according to pre-established schedules—before the food and supplies were loaded. The vans were inspected again when they arrived at the specially designated entry point at the Fleet Center. Inspection logs were maintained recording the drivers and deliveries.

Limos and Truck Rentals

Depending on the nature and importance of the special event, it may also be advisable to do background checks on all limo drivers and companies that will be used during the event. For the Republican National Convention, the NYPD received cooperation from regional rental companies with names of individuals renting trucks prior to the convention.

Mail/Express Mail

For selected major special events, security planners need to determine the extent to which the event venue needs to have mail and packages inspected prior to the event. The U.S. Postal Service, Inspection Service, will work with special event organizers to conduct pre-delivery screening of mail and packages (for explosives and biohazards, e.g., anthrax). This service is restricted to events where a threat assessment shows a high degree of risk. Organizers may also have to establish such services with private express mail delivery companies.

Physical Facilities Inspection

Prior to major special events, the lead law enforcement agency should ensure that the Fire Marshall or city/county building inspector has inspected all event venues. This inspection should include the areas listed below.

Physical facilities inspection areas:

* Are all alarms in working order?

* Are security doors and gates alarmed?

* In case of fire or evacuation, do doors automatically unlock?

* How are alarms monitored?

* Are emergency plans up to date?

* Do security planners have a floor plan?

* Are HVAC (heating, ventilation, and air conditioning), mechanical, gas, and other critical systems up to date?

Cash Security

At many special events, especially sporting events and concerts, thousands of dollars in cash may be collected at ticket booths, concession stands, and the like. Law enforcement overseeing security of the event is often responsible, sometimes in cooperation with private security, for protecting the cash collections. This protection includes securing the cash from external robbery but also from employee theft and loss.

Some issues that should be considered in securing cash collections at special events include the following:

- Have all cash collection booths and concessions been located and marked on the facility/ stadium floor plan map?

- Are security forces located near the cash collection and concession areas?

- Has law enforcement reviewed the travel routes that event staff will take to move cash to a central location?

- Have the travel routes for cash been reviewed for vulnerabilities?

- Has law enforcement reviewed and agreed to the pick-up times to collect the cash?

- Is the central cash location secured by law enforcement or private security?

- Does the central cash location contain a secure safe to store the cash until it is transported to a bank?

- Has law enforcement obtained a written estimate of the amount of cash that will be collected at each booth and concession?

- Does law enforcement have a list of names and duties for all personnel who will handle the cash?

- Does the event organizer contract with an armored vehicle service to pick up the cash and transport it to a bank?

4. Transportation/Traffic

Key Questions to Ask:

Do we have adequate security staffing and assignments for motorcades carrying VIPs?

Do we have adequate motorcade route plans and contingency route plans?

Have all personnel involved in motorcade security been briefed on the plans?

Do we have maps showing anticipated traffic patterns for spectators coming to and leaving the event?

Have we conducted risk assessments for all transportation modes—vehicle traffic, mass transit (buses, subways, trains), marine traffic, and more?

Vehicle Access

In developing security plans for major special events, the lead agency needs to consider all transportation modes that may have an impact on security of the event venue. In working with transportation officials, traffic engineering, fire/EMS, and others, the decision may be made to close streets, re-route traffic patterns, close transit stops, and the like for security purposes. While this causes an inconvenience to event participants, after the 1995 Oklahoma City bombing and 9/11, we realize that explosives can be transported to a special venue in a variety of transportation modes. As the Boston Police Commissioner responded when asked about rearranging parking at the Fleet Center, "The days where convention delegates could drive up to the convention center and get out at the curb are over."

Based on bomb blast analyses,[38] the Secret Service, city of Boston, Boston Police Department, U.S. Department of Transportation, and others decided to close Interstate 93 that runs adjacent to the Fleet Center while the Democratic National Convention was in progress. They also decided to close the MBTA train station under the Fleet Center. In contrast, the Secret Service, city of New York, NYPD, and others decided not to close the train station under Madison Square Garden, host to the Republican National Convention.

Lead agencies may need help from other agencies, the state, or the U.S. Coast Guard to assist with marine transportation security (possibly including dive teams). In a unique situation, at Super Bowl XXXIX in Jacksonville, Florida, in February 2005, the Sheriff's Office needed support to provide security to five cruise ships that served as supplemental hotels to Super Bowl participants.

Motorcades

The Secret Service places a heightened significance on the security of motorcades that are often part of major special events, for example, escorting VIPs or heads of state to and from airports. The history of assaults on "protectees" around the world while riding in, approaching, or leaving a motorcade should be considered when developing motorcade advance planning. Contemporary threats such as vehicle borne explosives, roadside improvised explosive devices, and unidentified aircraft over motorcade routes are all security issues that must be considered in the planning stages. While security planners should try and keep information about motorcade routes and times to those with a need to know, experience indicates that this is often difficult. Motorcade routes and times are often reported by local news media. Some security considerations for motorcades during special events are shown below.

Law enforcement should also publicize street closings, with times and locations, due to official motorcades.[39] This gives drivers an opportunity to avoid potential traffic delays, which could also affect the motorcade.

While there are many more details to motorcade security, any agency that requires special advice or training should contact the local Secret Service Special Agent in Charge (SAIC), since this is a specialty of the agency.

[38] See TSWG at www.tswg.gov/tswg/prods_pubs/CardSetPress.htm.

[39] See press release by Metro Nashville Police Department at www.police.nashville.org/news/media/2004/08/30.htm.

Exit Flow

While traffic to a major special event may arrive in a steady stream over a period of 1-8 hours or more depending on when the event opens the gates, nearly all the traffic attempts to exit at the same time when the event is over. Additionally, some security efforts may become more relaxed when the event has ended because agencies think their security job is over.

Efficient vehicle event exit flow is important to security and public relations. Some people may leave special events having consumed too much alcohol. Sitting in heavily congested traffic for a long period of time may contribute to road rage, which could contribute to accidents, disruptive behavior, and more. In addition, spectators may be reluctant to return to some special events if they experienced long delays in leaving an event.

Agencies need to plan for efficient and effective traffic flow exiting special events. Traffic engineering specialists and the state police can be helpful in moving vehicle traffic swiftly and safely after an event. For example, the state police used one of the Interstate 93 northbound lanes for southbound traffic (and separated the lanes with safety cones) leaving the New Hampshire International Speedway after a NASCAR race.

Event security planners need to prepare travel and security plans for motorcades that include the following considerations:

- Do we have adequate staffing and post assignments?

- Have all security staff been briefed on the motorcade plans?

- Do we have secure vehicles to transport VIPs (swept and inspected)?

- Do we have adequate security vehicles surrounding the VIP vehicles (e.g., cruisers, motorcycles)?

- Are motorcade communications on a separate channel so they can be in constant communication with each other?

- Are command post personnel monitoring the motorcade communications channel?

- Have we blocked off and secured critical intersections on the travel route?

- Do we have tow trucks on standby to clear blocked routes?

- What considerations have we given to spectators or bystanders along the routes?

- Have we done adequate counter-surveillance on the traffic route to look for suspicious vehicles, rooftop/tower/overpass vantage points, and other vulnerable areas?

Special Traffic Problems

Events like Cinco de Mayo and Mardi Gras traditionally involve some form of "cruising" that creates extra traffic and safety problems. As part of planning and managing Cinco de Mayo in Denver, for example, police meet with event representatives to establish ground rules for cruising. Several police departments surveyed expressed dismay over the Mardi Gras practice of women in cars "flashing for beads." Law enforcement needs to find creative ways in the event planning stages to deal with such special traffic problems.

The Philadelphia Police Department encounters problems with "cruisers" at the annual Greek Picnic and other outdoor special events. To manage this problem, they employ barricades on designated streets to route the cruisers away from the event area and disrupt the flow of cruising. Small mobile units of motorcycle officers react to the constantly changing cruising patterns by erecting new barricades and removing others.

Aircraft/Helicopter Access and Airspace Protection

For some larger special events, law enforcement needs to be concerned about aircraft flying overhead, e.g., small aircraft towing advertisement banners. Since 9/11, the "Black Sunday"[40] scenario is a real possibility for major special events held in stadiums.

After 9/11, the Federal Aviation Administration (FAA), with advice from the Transportation Security Administration (TSA), began to issue more temporary flight restrictions (TFRs) over major special events, especially stadiums used for the National Football League, Major League Baseball, large NCAA football games (e.g., Division I), and large NASCAR events. Typical TFRs restrict small aircraft from flying within three miles from the center of the stadium and below 3,000 feet above ground level. However, the FAA (and TSA) could issue waivers for small aircraft (like aerial advertisers). In February 2003, the U.S. Congress limited this waiver authority and specifically barred aerial advertisers from receiving TFR waivers.[41]

Another concern is the security at small airports that are located in close proximity to major event stadiums. TSA plans to issue a set of "best practices" and recommended guidelines to improve security at general aviation airports, and a self-assessment guide for general aviation airport managers to use. [42] Law enforcement agencies planning major special events should meet with local airport managers and review their security plans.

Some larger events, like NASCAR races, also draw a number of helicopter landings and takeoffs (usually transporting VIPs) within the stadium infield. These aircraft and flights are usually managed by private services that have their own dispatching and flight control. Law enforcement agencies planning major special events that involve helicopter flights should meet with the services and establish security guidelines.

Only for very large and significant special events, such as NSSEs, would lead security agencies plan for airspace protection, surveillance, and interdiction. Because of the nature of these events, involving the President or foreign heads of state, security would be managed largely by federal agencies.

[40] See Harris, Thomas, *Black Sunday*. Penguin Putnam Inc., 1975. This fictional book describes an attempt by a terrorist to drop a bomb from a blimp over the Super Bowl in New Orleans.

[41] Consolidated Appropriations Resolution, 2003, P.L. 108-7, Section 352. In January 2004, Congress passed legislation continuing this restriction indefinitely, Consolidated Appropriations Act, 2004, P.L. 108-199, Section 521.

[42] General Accounting Office letter on aviation security to DHS Secretary dated March 5, 2004.

5. Law Enforcement Intelligence

Key Questions to Ask:

Does the lead agency have an effective intelligence capability?

Can we receive support from a state agency with an intelligence capability?

Can we receive support from, or assign an officer to, the local FBI Joint Terrorism Task Force (JTTF)?

Do state and local law enforcement need security clearances?

Do we have adequate intelligence support to conduct threat and risk assessments?

Do we need to employ intelligence resources in the field during the event?

Massachusetts Governor Mitt Romney, former head of the 2002 Salt Lake City Olympics organizing committee, attributed the primary reason for the success of security at the Olympic games to the intense intelligence efforts behind the scenes. The Governor noted that "intelligence work in the nation as a whole is the key to protecting the homeland."[43]

The best intelligence comes from a variety of sources—law enforcement (federal, state, local); community; businesses; news media; criminals; and others. Police across the world are now finding that there may be a connection between investigating everyday local crime (e.g., call from neighbors about unusual noise or smell in an apartment) and a terrorist cell planning an operation. Common local crimes (e.g., cigarette smuggling) may also be part of front activities to funnel money to terrorist cells.

As noted in a recent COPS Office publication, community-policing partnerships "can be invaluable in the prevention of terrorist activity because they can result in increased intelligence sharing."[44] Law enforcement agencies need to be familiar with legal issues and requirements related to intelligence collection and storage.[45]

The lead agency should begin contacting intelligence sources many months before a major special event to alert them to pass on any information pertinent to the upcoming event. The role of intelligence gathering prior to a major special event has grown in importance in this era of terrorist threats against the U.S.

For NSSEs and other federally-managed major events, the FBI is the lead federal agency for intelligence. The FBI has developed a robust "Concept of Operations" for managing intelligence related to special events that entails coverage of the entire intelligence cycle, including establishment of requirements, collection, analysis, production, and dissemination. Representatives from local FBI field offices, which each contain an interagency Field Intelligence Group (FIG), may be integrated into planning and operations for major events. If state and local officers are participating in special event security with federal agencies, they may need security clearances to receive intelligence information or serve as liaisons for a Federal Operations Center.

Chief Inspector Joseph O'Connor, Counterterrorism Unit Commander, Philadelphia Police Department, provided the following observations regarding intelligence considerations for special event planning:

> We perform a threat assessment with help from the FBI before every major event. We have found the FBI to be very cooperative. We are interested in intelligence that is pertinent to Philadelphia and the region. Intelligence is very important in planning for special events. Since 9/11, we pay very close attention to the international situation when planning for special events. Every lead and piece of information must be investigated thoroughly, no matter how fantastic or improbable it might appear.

The intelligence process related to special events should be viewed as (1) pre-event intelligence—help in planning, and (2) intelligence during the event—help in managing the event.

[43] United Press International, July 14, 2004.

[44] See Scheider et al, *Connecting the Dots for a Proactive Approach*, Office of Community Oriented Policing Services, U.S. Department of Justice, p. 162, www.cops.usdoj.gov/mime/open.pdf?Item=1046.

[45] See the COPS Office's *Law Enforcement Tech Guide: How to Plan, Purchase, and Manage Technology (Successfully!)* at www.cops.usdoj.gov.

Pre-Event Intelligence

In the special event planning stage, the intelligence planning group or subcommittee is one of the most important planning resources. This group should serve as a resource for information and intelligence to practically every other planning subcommittee.

The intelligence resources can assist with conducting threat and risk assessments, providing special intelligence bulletins, and researching specific vulnerable situations. Intelligence staff can also help establish contact with telephone companies to assist with trap and trace services in the event of a telephoned bomb threat.

Many major local law enforcement agencies have adequate internal intelligence capabilities.[46] Agencies without adequate intelligence capabilities, or just to supplement their own capabilities, might partner with state agencies that have intelligence units or newly developing intelligence fusion centers.[47] For example, the Georgia Bureau of Identification's intelligence unit played a significant support role at the recent G-8 Summit in Sea Island, Georgia. In addition to state agencies, local agencies can turn to the FBI's Joint Terrorism Task Forces (JTTF) and the FIGs for intelligence support. The Secret Service can assist with intelligence on dangerous subjects who have made threats against public officials.

The Seattle Police Department has shared with law enforcement, in its After Action Report on the 1999 WTO meeting protestor riots, that the pre-event "intelligence assessments were not integrated into the planning process in a timeframe that allowed the depth of comprehensive contingency planning." The department went on to recommend in its report:

> It is necessary to carefully assess the importance of preliminary intelligence information, with appropriate caveats, and for commanders to use this information to identify and plan for the full range of contingencies to include "worst-case" scenarios.[48]

A common intelligence source that law enforcement has used to gain information on groups trying to disrupt special events is the Internet. In planning security for a 2002 World Trade Organization meeting in Washington, D.C., Metropolitan Police Department intelligence officers monitored demonstrators' web sites to learn about planned disruptive, and sometimes illegal, activities. When the groups arrived on site, police also infiltrated the membership. Information from these sources helped police stay ahead of troublesome behavior. In planning security for the Tulsa, Oklahoma, State Fair, Tulsa County Sheriff's deputies gained information from a web site that about 100 youth planned to "blow a whistle, then run like crazy" to incite the crowd to run as well. To prevent this, the deputies zoned the area so that no one could run more than about 10 yards without encountering an officer.

Intelligence During the Event

At the beginning stage of an event, part of the intelligence capability that is dedicated to the event should move to the central communications command center, while the main intelligence resources remain in a centralized location. Intelligence officers should provide daily briefings to command center personnel. Briefing times should be posted so command center staff know when to expect them. Intelligence staff might also prepare "lookout" reports that provide photos of suspicious persons (e.g., made comments regarding the event, showed unusual "interest" in the event, etc.). Intelligence officers or investigators also help investigate leads during the event.

For example, some agencies, such as NYPD, have an ongoing terrorist "hotline" that citizens can call to report suspicious behavior. If any of the tips appear like legitimate leads and are connected to the special event, the intelligence staff can conduct immediate follow-up investigations.

[46] See Carter, David, *Law Enforcement Intelligence: A Guide for State, Local, and Tribal Law Enforcement Agencies* at www.cops.usdoj.gov/mime/open.pdf?Item=1392.

[47] See http://it.ojp.gov.

[48] See Seattle Police Department, *After Action Report, World Trade Organization Ministerial Conference, November 29-December 3, 1999.*

The event security planners should decide in advance if intelligence officers are needed in the field. This may often be helpful if the event involves planned demonstrations and protest movements. Field intelligence also helps with counter surveillance at major events.

After 9/11, the Indianapolis Police Department began stationing intelligence officers at the command post for large special events, as well as in the field. This is part of an overall effort in the department to do "more aggressive real-time monitoring" of gang activity and other potential threats to public safety. Officers in the field are expected to report various types of suspicious activity to the command post intelligence officers. For example, they might report observing an unusually large number of cars with license plates from a particular state. Although this might not turn out to be significant, on the other hand it might fit with other available intelligence and help identify a threat.

Decisions often have to be made during special events concerning when and how to act on intelligence information. For example, just before the start of the Democratic National Convention in Boston, the FBI advised the media that the agency was investigating "unconfirmed information" of a possible attack on media during the DNC. The FBI Boston Field Office issued the following statement: "The FBI has received unconfirmed information that a domestic group is planning to disrupt the DNC by attacking media vehicles with explosives or incendiary devices." The FBI stated that they were notifying the media because they were potential targets.

In San Diego County, the Sheriff's Department re-routed RV parking away from the county fairgrounds during the recent state fair based on intelligence about potential terrorist activity associated with an RV.

Event planners should also consider sending e-mails to local businesses to tell them about protestor demonstration plans that might cause property damage to their businesses. While not trying to cause panic, this information allows businesses to take precautions to avert property damage.

6. Credentialing

Key Questions to Ask:

Do we have a plan and process to produce credentials for the special event?

Do we have adequate technology to produce credentials?

Do we have the required personnel contact information in a database to produce credentials?

If we don't have the capacity to produce credentials in-house, what agency can we partner with to help us?

[49] U.S. Secret Service training module entitled *Major Events Credentialing*, 2004.

The Secret Service notes the following in its training regarding the mission of major events credentialing:

> The mission of major events credentialing is to design and produce badge identification to ensure the greatest possible level of security for personnel and property, and to enhance the ability of law enforcement to control access to secure areas, facilities, and events.[49]

Because proper credentialing can be very expensive, some special event organizers cut corners on this task. They sometimes don't conduct proper background checks on personnel and don't invest in badges that can't be counterfeited.

The Secret Service stresses the difference between a "credential" and a "ticket." A credential identifies specific individuals who are allowed access to a venue for a purpose. A ticket is issued to spectators or the general public. Security staff should not confuse the two. A ticket to enter an event is not a credential—you cannot assume that someone with a ticket has been vetted for security purposes.

Badges are typically color-coded to show perimeter access. For example, referring back to Exhibit 2, a purple badge may allow access to the middle perimeter and red allows access to the inner perimeter. All security personnel should receive briefing packets that show the badge colors and explain the access codes. For most major special events, photo identification is also part of the badge.

Color-coding might also be used to designate functions of personnel: blue equals law enforcement, green for government staff, orange for VIPs and dignitaries, etc.

Using credentials also allows security planners to create zones within perimeters. In other words, security can allow someone access to the inner perimeter but still restrict them from having access to VIPs, performers, etc. At NASCAR races, some people are issued color-coded credentials that allow them access to the infield, so they can walk around and see the drivers and their RVs; however, they are restricted from actually walking around the "pits" unless they have a special badge.

Badges can also identify who is law enforcement, who is allowed to carry a firearm, who has escort privileges, and more.

The two parts of credentialing that are costly are doing background checks on personnel who are issued badges and badge technology.

Event security planners may need to run background checks (at a minimum, National Crime Information Center (NCIC) checks) on some people being granted inner perimeter access depending on the nature of the event and the VIPs in attendance (political figures, foreign heads of state, etc.). For example, if an event is held in a hotel, can hotel management verify that they have had local law enforcement run a background check on a waiter with inner perimeter access? Has the waiter worked for the hotel for many years? If the waiter is new and no background check was done, security staff should conduct one if that person will be given a badge to the inner perimeter.

The technology involves cameras to take photo identification, computers to store contact information, and badge-making equipment. Sophisticated badge-making equipment and software involves placing holographs on the badges so that they are difficult to counterfeit. In the future, event badges may also include some biometric identification and bar coding.

Some tips and considerations for credentialing at special events include:

- Provide adequate information on badges to verify the identity of wearers and their level of access.

- Make codes easy for security personnel to interpret.

- Include enough security features to prevent counterfeiting and assist in credential verification.

- Who will get credentialed?

- Which credentialed personnel require police background records checks?

- Who will conduct the records checks?

- What criteria will be used to exclude people from receiving badges?

- Who will handle credential production?

- How will credentials be distributed?

- Where will the credentialing center be located (must be open prior to and during event)?

7. Administrative and Logistics Support

Key Questions to Ask:

Do we have a designated administrative logistics coordinator?

Have we developed a task list and timeline to manage the administrative and logistical needs?

Do we have an adequate inventory of needed equipment, supplies, and other items to provide security at the special event?

Which other agencies can we work with to borrow or lease needed equipment, vehicles, and other logistical support items?

Are we prepared to make timely purchases of any equipment or supplies that we need to acquire for the event?

Do we have an adequate budget to support the security needs of the special event?

Administrative and logistical support for security at major special events is critically important to the success of the event. This support begins in the early planning stages and continues after the event has concluded.

One of the earliest considerations for the lead law enforcement agency is the adequacy of the finances to provide security to the event. Adequate funding is required for event planning, training, payment of overtime, purchase of equipment and supplies, and more. Based on a review of security needs and specifications for the upcoming event, a security budget should be prepared early in the planning process.

At the beginning of the event security planning process, the lead agency should designate an "administrative logistics coordinator." This person would be given the authority to oversee the integration and coordination of all administrative and logistical support in terms of event security.

Early in the process, this coordinator needs to contact each security planning team (subcommittee) and distribute a form that requests each team's needs in terms of equipment, supplies, and other logistical support. This will help in coordinating among planning teams—for example, eliminating duplication of equipment.

It will also help to establish a timeline and task chart for managing all administrative and logistical functions. It can take many months to purchase certain types of equipment going through most government procurement processes.[50] For the G-8 Summit in Georgia, some riot gear that was ordered did not arrive in time for the mobile teams to train with the equipment.

This coordinator will have to be adept at working with city, county, state, and possibly federal financial officials for some major events. Some events, because of size and political importance, are eligible for outside funding support (e.g., grants or cost-reimbursement from federal agencies), which has to be carefully accounted for.

The administrative and logistics coordinator also needs to be able to develop partnerships with other agencies (local, state, federal) to determine if needed equipment can be borrowed, leased, or provided in some other way. Regional authorities, such as Councils of Government (COG) sometimes have equipment (e.g., radios) that can be borrowed. Coordinators might also check with state departments of homeland security, state police, FEMA, the DHS Special Event program, and local offices for the FBI, Secret Service, and ATF. In addition, the Department of Defense can provide administrative and/or logistical support to special events under qualifying circumstances.

The administrative and logistical needs for security at special events can be divided into three areas: operational logistics, administrative support, and specialized support. Each will be discussed below.

[50]See the COPS Office's *Law Enforcement Tech Guide: How to Plan, Purchase, and Manage Technology (Successfully)* at www.cops.usdoj.gov.

Operational Logistics

Operational logistics involves support for security-related needs in the field— getting personnel resources to the field, equipping them, housing and feeding them, and attending to their other needs. Illustrations of operational logistics:

- Transporting personnel to the field and posts may involve use of vans, buses, and other transportation.

- Parking for security personnel.

- Lodging for security personnel, if needed. Lodging the security forces from the many outside agencies at the G-8 Summit in Georgia required thousands of hotel rooms.

- Food and beverages for the security forces in the field and at fixed posts.

- At the G-8 Summit in Georgia, over 270,000 meals were served and over 16,000 cases of bottled water were distributed.

- Tents (air conditioned) for breaks and meals. Many security events are held outside in hot summer months. In addition to providing water and meals to security forces, event organizers should provide air conditioned tents for shade and rest breaks.

- Bathrooms. Organizers may have to provide portable bathrooms for security forces for outside events.

- Security equipment. This will often include security fences, jersey barriers, hazmat clothing, riot gear, magnetometers, etc.

- Specialized equipment. This may include generators, portable radios, towers, and other large items.

- Specialized transport equipment. This may include bicycles, scooters, golf carts, motorcycles, explosive transport vehicles, and the like.

- Supplies. This may include credentialing supplies and ordinary office supplies.

Administrative Support

Administrative support involves support related to acquiring and purchasing equipment and other items, tracking costs, and more. Examples of administrative support include the following:

- Purchasing equipment and supplies.

- Paying overtime to lead agency personnel.

- Reimbursing personnel expenses to other partner agencies.

- Tracking costs and equipment. Place identification tags on all equipment and create an online inventory showing who checked the equipment out.

- Acquiring (e.g., renting) space, facilities, storage facilities for security purposes, and more.

- Acquiring and providing computers, cell phones, phones, and other communications resources.

Specialized Support

Specialized support can involve a variety of special services. A common example is video support. The Philadelphia Police Department's audiovisual unit attends many of the special events secured by the agency in order to take video and still photos for historical and security purposes.

8. Protecting Critical Infrastructure and Utilities

Key Questions to Ask:

Have we conducted risk assessments on critical infrastructure and utilities that

could impact the special event?

Have we collaborated with infrastructure and utilities managers to develop

adequate security plans?

Have we coordinated with sanitation services for event security support?

Have we considered protective measures for cyber systems in event of attack?

In planning for major event security, the lead agency needs to carefully consider and plan to protect critical infrastructure and utilities. For major events, this function may be a separate planning team; for smaller events, the function might be part of another team's responsibilities.

All risks to major infrastructure and utilities (e.g., contamination of the water supply) should be assessed and considered in developing the event security plan. The lead agency needs to coordinate with other agencies and review security plans for infrastructure and utilities that could threaten the security of the special event such as the local water supply, water treatment facilities, electricity supply, communications grid, sewer system, and more.

Coordination with and support from city or county sanitation services can also be very helpful in planning security for special events. At some special events, manhole covers have been welded shut near the event venues. Many security agencies also have newspaper dispensers and public trashcans removed prior to the event, especially events that are attended by protest groups. Bombs can be placed in these receptacles, they can be used as missiles and thrown at law enforcement, or they can be used to damage other property (e.g., thrown through store windows).

Law enforcement and government officials should work with the media to alert citizens to the security justifications for inconveniencing them by removing newspaper dispensers and public trashcans. At the 2004 Democratic National Convention, the Boston Police Department and the city removed public trashcans about a week prior to the start of the event (agencies can't wait until the last minute to do everything; some things must be done earlier than others). Some of the affected public complained to the media.

Cyber Security

As stated earlier in these guidelines, one of the greatest potential threats to special event security may be a cyber attack. The National Infrastructure Advisory Council has noted that cyber vulnerability may lead to "an implicit or explicit failure of the confidentiality, integrity, or availability of an information system."[51] The fear is that a group could disrupt a major special event by infiltrating or hacking into on site information systems that control communications, utilities (electricity, water, heating, cooling), or other essential information technology.

As previously mentioned in the section on cyber vulnerability, the Secret Service has been leading the effort to develop cyber security for major special events. The Secret Service has developed a partnership with the Carnegie Mellon University Software Engineering Institute's CERT® Coordination Center (CERT/CC).[52] The Center is developing protocols to evaluate information technology security risks and implement protective measures.

Under the Secret Services' leadership and partnership with the Center, law enforcement can expect helpful information, guidance, and practices in the future regarding cyber security for special events.

At the local level, security agencies should consider protective measures for cyber systems. In developing contingency plans, security officials should develop plans in case an event is targeted. Efforts should involve mitigating the impact of the cyber attack and continuing services (back up/alternate plans for essential services). In order to obtain technical expertise to manage these cyber issues, local law enforcement may need to partner with universities or the private sector.

9. Fire/EMS/Hospitals/Public Health

Key Questions to Ask:

Do we give adequate consideration in our security planning to detecting threats from explosives and from radiological, chemical, and biological agents?

Do we have adequate management and response plans for these threats?

Do we have adequate protocols for handling bomb threats?

Do we have an adequate emergency evacuation plan?

Fire and emergency medical services (EMS) play a critical role in supporting security and public safety at special events. Additionally, hospital medical care must be adequately available if needed. Fire, EMS, and medical care should be a separate planning team, chaired by the chief fire/EMS service in the jurisdiction hosting the special event. But the plans must be integrated into the overall security plan for the event. As noted earlier, the role of the fire marshal (city, county, or state) is also critically important to conduct safety inspections of special event venues, key hotels, and other facilities involved in the event prior to the event.

Fire and EMS agencies will have specific needs at the event, such as stand-by and staging areas for fire apparatus, ambulances, and special operations vehicles (such as hazmat vehicles); access to critical infrastructure, e.g., sprinkler connections, fire hydrants, utility panels; and entry and egress routes for emergency vehicles. Isolation of these agencies from the security and perimeter planning will lead to potentially significant hindrances in caring for the public in the event of an emergency incident during the special event.

Hospitals should also be integrated into the overall security plan in order to provide critical information to these primary health care facilities on anticipated threats and attendance to the event. Public health agencies should be included in planning sessions to assist them in preparation for potential hazmat/WMD situations that may impact the community.

51 See National Infrastructure Advisory Council's *Vulnerability Disclosure Framework*, www.dhs.gov/xlibrary/assets/vdwgreport.pdf and *The National Strategy to Secure Cyberspace*, White House Report, Office of the President, Washington, DC, www.whitehouse.gov/pcipb.

52 See www.cert.org.

At special events with a potential for attracting civil disturbances or arson incidents, some law enforcement agencies partner with fire/EMS to create special fire tactical units that respond as a team, including police escorts. In some large cities, such as Philadelphia, these tactical fire units often consist of ladder trucks, engines, EMS, and fire command personnel with a police escort—at least two police vehicles/minimum of eight police officers. The entire tactical unit moves as a team. The police escorts never leave the fire units to answer other calls for service. Their sole duty is the protection of fire personnel. Fire and EMS services, in collaboration with the lead security agency, need to assess the nature of the event and determine, among others, some of the key issues listed below.

Fire and EMS services also need to help the event organizers identify and coordinate with the main trauma center hospital to transport event participants that become ill or injured during the event. Depending on the size and nature of the event, the hospital should agree to be prepared to implement their emergency management and disaster plans.

Key issues for fire/EMS to consider in providing public safety at special events include the following:

- What numbers and types of personnel are needed at the event—on standby?

- What types of apparatus, medical vehicles, and equipment are needed at the event?

- Where should vehicles and personnel be placed at the event?

- Are floors plans (showing electrical, HVAC systems, etc.) available for event facilities?

- Do event facilities (stadiums, arenas, etc.) have adequate evacuation plans?

- What is the primary trauma center hospital that will be used during the event?

---

10. Hazardous Materials/Weapons of Mass Destruction: Detection, Response, and Management

Key Questions to Ask:

Have we developed adequate plans for fire and EMS services' response if needed at the event?

What numbers and types of personnel are needed at the event?

What types of apparatus, medical vehicles, and equipment are needed at the event?

Have we coordinated adequately with a hospital to handle any casualties?

Major special events, which draw a variety of VIPs, thousands of spectators, media, and others, can be targets for terrorists. In May 2004, Akhmad Kadyrov, the Russian-backed civilian administrator of Chechnya, and 30 other people were killed when a bomb exploded under the VIP reviewing stand in Grozny, Russia, during Victory Day observances (celebrating the defeat of Germany in WWII). Security at the stadium was very tight and explosive detection canines had reportedly swept the reviewing stand area prior to the event.[53] In 1996 at the Olympics in Atlanta, a bomb was detonated in Centennial Olympic Park that killed one person and injured many others. On May 10, 2005, when President Bush was addressing a crowd at Freedom Square in the Georgian capital of Tbilisi, someone tossed a live grenade into the crowd, about 100 feet from the stage where the President was standing.[54]

The United States' main terrorist threat, Al Qaeda, has long shown an interest in acquiring or developing biological and chemical weapons. In testimony before the 9/11 Commission in March 2004, former CIA Director George Tenet cited Al Qaeda manuals in warning of a "heightened risk of poison attacks" in the near future. Tenet went on to note:

> Extremists have widely disseminated instructions for a chemical weapon using common materials that could cause large numbers of casualties in a crowded, enclosed area.[55]

In planning security for major special events, law enforcement must always consider the risk from hazardous materials and weapons of mass destruction. As discussed in this section, hazmat will include weapons of mass destruction. As described by the FBI, planning for hazmat incidents during special events focuses on four primary objectives: (1) availability of subject matter experts (SMEs) for rapid risk assessment of received threats, (2) procedures for venue protection from hazmat, (3) development of assessment teams for reported hazmat incidents in and around the venues, and (4) response and protective actions for law enforcement in the event of a hazmat incident. FBI protocols for these threats at major special events are described below.

[53] Associated Press, May 9, 2004.

[54] "FBI: Grenade Was a Threat to Bush," *The Washington Post*, May 19, 2005.

[55] Warrick, Joby, "Al Qaeda Chemist and the Quest for Ricin," *The Washington Post*, May 5, 2004, A-1.

Current Threats

Current threats from hazmat include: explosives, industrial chemicals, biological toxins, biological pathogens, radiological sources, "military" chemical weapons, and nuclear devices.

- Explosives: Explosives statistically remain the most likely form of terrorist use of hazmat against the public. The ease of acquisition of explosives, and chemicals that may be crafted into explosives, as well as the knowledge base present among potential terrorist groups and individuals, or ease of access to the knowledge, make Improvised Explosive Devices (IED's) a major threat during special events.

- Chemicals: Toxic industrial chemicals (TIC) are readily accessible to potential terrorist groups and individuals, either by theft from transportation or industrial sources, purchase of TICs, or by targeting industrial installations near the event venue site. Due to their ease of acquisition, sheer volume in industry and transportation, and the chemical and physical properties of many of these TICs, they present a greater threat to special events than many of the military chemical warfare agents (CWA) such as sarin (nerve agent) and sulfur mustard (blister agent). Some agents, such as chlorine, phosgene, and hydrogen cyanide, are both TICs and CWAs, and present significant threats for special events.

- Biological: Release of biological agents at special events presents special risks, in that the release may be covert in nature and not detected until human "indicators" arrive in hospitals, doctor's offices, and public health clinics several days after exposure at the event. Biological agents may take the form of either biologic toxins, such as ricin or clostridium botulinum; or biologic pathogens, including bacteria such as bacillus anthracis (anthrax), viruses such as variola major (smallpox), rickettsia, fungi, and others.

- Radiological: Use of radiological materials at a special event may occur in one of three basic scenarios: distribution of radioactive sources, use of radioactive sources in conjunction with explosives or mechanical means of dispersal (a radiological dispersal device or RDD), or a nuclear device. Of these potential scenarios, the use of radiological sources, either alone or in conjunction with an RDD, is the more likely event. Radiological screening at event venue entry points is useful to intercept these materials, however, traditional radiological monitoring tends to focus on detection of gamma radiation, and may miss pure alpha or beta radiological sources.

Threat Assessments

Planning for major special events must include consultation with subject matter experts (SMEs) experienced with dealing with threats from hazardous materials. It is likely that potential threats may be conveyed to the incident commander during the event.

The incident commander should have resources immediately available to assess these threats. A timely assessment will assist the incident commander in identifying responses appropriate to the threat level.

At the Federal level, responsibility for conducting threat assessments is identified in the National Response Plan as a function of the FBI (NRP Terrorism Incident Law Enforcement and Investigation Annex page TER-11). During major events such as NSSE's, a hazmat/WMD desk is established within the JOC, and is staffed by personnel from the FBI Hazardous Materials Response Unit.

Additional SME's from other appropriate local, state, and federal agencies are included as needed to address the threats received. The DHS Science and Technology Directorate, as the coordinating agency for scientific and technology support annex to the NRP, includes a wide variety of subject matter experts to support the FBI in this area.

Venue Protection

Protection from hazmat at venue entry portals may include detection devices for explosive residue, radiological detection, and portable chemical monitors—in numerous configurations, capabilities, and sensitivity levels. An important step for the planners of special events is to develop policy and procedure for actions to be followed in the event of positive reaction from these devices. It may be easy to strap radiation pagers on security staff assigned an entry screening detail, but what will happen when a patron comes through screening who has just completed medical treatment involving radiological isotopes? The officers on these details must have clear and concise guidance and training on how to proceed with using the detection devices to rule out non-threatening radiation sources, when to call for more advanced detection equipment, and who to call if any questions arise.

Likewise, the placement of detection and monitoring equipment within an event venue must be coordinated with the agencies having primary response jurisdiction for the venue in the event of a hazmat incident.

Assessment Teams

Placement of assessment teams inside the venue has become standard procedure for major special events managed by federal agencies. Joint Hazardous Materials Assessment Teams (JHAT) and Joint Hazardous Explosive Response Teams (JHERT) have been developed for response to reported hazmat and explosive threats or incidents in and around the venues. The JHATs and JHERTs consist of experienced personnel from different disciplines and levels of government, co-located in a single discreet response vehicle, ATV, or in a walking unit. The JHATs and JHERTs provide the incident commander a low-profile team that can unobtrusively assess the need for further specialized assets, allowing those valuable assets to remain available for actual incidents. Depending on the need for high level security at the event, a Bomb Management Center (BMC) may be part of the assessment team process. The BMC oversees the response of all explosive-related assets to include the coordinated response of the JHERT.

JHATs are typically configured with federal, state and local hazmat personnel. These personnel are experienced in hazmat response, and have authority within their organizations to make decisions regarding the assessment of potential hazmat materials. At high-level FBI SERL events, the federal hazmat position is normally staffed by a Hazardous Materials Officer from the FBI Hazardous Materials Response Unit (HMRU), as the FBI is the lead investigative agency for acts of terrorism involving hazmat. At NSSE event venues, an additional federal hazmat position is filled by the U.S. Secret Service, as the Secret Service is the lead agency for security at NSSEs. The local agency providing primary hazmat response in the community, typically the fire department, fills a position in the JHAT, and the last position in the JHAT may be either state/local law enforcement hazmat, or state national guard civil support team personnel. The JHAT also carries a basic detection and monitoring capability. Most importantly, the JHAT carries a communication capability for each agency represented, and experienced personnel who can collectively assess potential hazmat threats—advising the event incident commander that the threat is either not credible and no threat, or legitimate in nature and in need of further resources. Actions of the JHAT are controlled by the hazmat desk located within the Joint Operations Center (JOC).

Some key issues to consider concerning detecting and responding to hazmat situations at special events include the following:

- Is the threat to the event great enough to acquire and employ advanced technology? For some major events, the Philadelphia Police Department equips supervisors with radiation detectors that they wear during the event (e.g., recent 4th of July event).

- If advanced detection technology is warranted, can collaborative partners, such as federal agencies, provide the equipment? For example, at magnetometer access points, to swab bags with sensor pads and examine the swabs with explosive detection machines.[*]

- Have all collaborative partners been identified and are they working together?

- Have we consulted with appropriate federal resources?

- Besides specialists, how many police officers should be equipped with PPE? What level of PPE and hazmat training should we provide to officers and supervisors? The NYPD has developed a useful course entitled Chemical, Ordinance, Biological, and Radiological Awareness (COBRA) training. For the 2004 Republican National Convention, thousands of officers received this training. They also provide field officers with training from the 2004 Emergency Response Guidebook, which is a guide to aid first responders in (1) quickly identifying the specific or generic classification of the hazardous material involved in the incident, and (2) protecting themselves and the public during this initial response phase of the incident.[**]

- Have we identified immediate evacuation routes for non-hazmat certified personnel in the event of a hazmat incident?

- Have we identified SMEs that will assist with hazmat threat assessments?

- Have we contacted the local field division of the FBI in the event we need the capability to process contaminated crime scenes for evidence? What about ATF?

- Have joint training exercises been conducted?

- Does the plan involve establishing response protocols for the first officers on the scene (e.g., setting up control and safety zones, developing a triage system, etc.)?

- Does plan include locations, equipment, and staff to decontaminate persons exposed to chemicals and other substances (e.g., pepper spray)?

[*] In an example of a public-private partnership, a new airborne contaminants detection system was tested at Churchill Downs during the 2004 Kentucky Derby.

[**] See www.osha.gov/dts/osta/bestpractices/html/hospital_firstreceivers.html. See also, the National Institute of Justice, U.S. Department of Justice's CD entitled Emergency Responder Chemical and Biological Equipment Guides and Database. Provides a searchable database to help in the evaluation and purchase of chemical and biological detection and personal protective equipment. See also, OSHA hazmat training levels at 29 C.F.R. 1910.120 (q)(6).

Response and Protective Actions

A key part of hazmat planning at major special events involves developing a response plan to hazmat situations and also concerns the use and training involved in personal protective equipment (PPE) and advance detection and monitoring equipment. The response plan must include measures to protect emergency responders and public safety; restore essential government services; and provide emergency relief to governments, businesses, and people affected by the terrorist act. Under the National Response Plan, FEMA can request resources from many other federal agencies to support local governments overwhelmed by an emergency.[56] The Department of Homeland Security's Office of State and Local Government Coordination and Preparedness and FEMA both provide training to help local jurisdictions develop plans.[57]

Wearing PPE (e.g., chemical protective clothing, respiratory protection) requires compliance with numerous standards (e.g., Occupational Safety and Health Administration's Hazardous Waste Operations and Emergency Response, 29 C.F.R. 1910.134, Respiratory Protection). This standard requires that personnel who respond to hazmat incidents must be trained to the hazardous materials operational level for defensive operations, and to the hazardous materials technician level for offensive operations. It further defines such essentials and medical monitoring, site safety, site operations, and other critical components. Simply handing an officer an air purifying respirator with the intent for its use in a hazmat incident, without medical evaluation, fit-testing and training would be a potential violation of OSHA regulations, and a threat to the officer's safety.

Also, having untrained personnel operate advanced detection and monitoring equipment may result in false interpretations of detector results, and subsequently inappropriate response actions based on those results.

Law enforcement agencies involved in planning major special events should also evaluate the capability of their tactical assault teams to operate in hazardous environments. If the capability does not exist locally, agencies should outreach to state and federal law enforcement for this capability.

Additionally, plans for the processing of contaminated crime scenes must be addressed. Primary responsibility for the collection of evidence from terrorism incidents falls to the FBI, through its hazardous materials response unit (HMRU). HMRU deploys supervisory special agents, hazmat officers, scientists, and field division hazardous materials response team (HMRT) personnel to major events and NSSEs for the purpose of processing contaminated crime scenes. HMRU will use other local, state, and federal law enforcement agencies with trained hazmat personnel as needed to assist in the evidence recovery operation. ATF's National Response Teams are also trained and capable of as-siting in processing these scenes.

As part of threat and risk assessments, discussed earlier, the lead agency should conduct extensive site observations and surveys. These assessments include identifying all venues, traffic routes, facilities, grounds, parking areas, etc. that need to be secured and protected. These facilities need to be examined in terms of vulnerabilities to the release of hazmat agents and bomb attacks.[58] The Technical Support Working Group has developed a set of guidelines that estimate the effects of a bomb on a structure and personnel in the structure.[59] The ATF has also developed lethal blast ranges for car and truck bombs, at which death can occur, and "minimum evacuation distances" for car and truck bombs, at which life-threatening injuries can be minimized. For example, a full-size sedan can be packed with approximately 1,000 pounds of explosives in the trunk. The lethal blast range when this car bomb is detonated is a radius of 125 feet; the minimum evacuation distance is 1,750 feet.

[56] See www.dhs.gov/interweb/assetlibrary/NRPbaseplan.pdf.

[57] See www.ojp.usdoj.gov/odp/docs/comnet.htm and www.training.fema.gov/emiweb/terrorismInfo/termng.asp. See National Fire Protection Association *NFPA 1600: Standard on Disaster/Emergency Management and Business Continuity* at www.nfpa.org/assets/files/PDF/NFPA1600.pdf.

[58] See National Institute for Occupational Safety and Health, *Guidance for Protecting Building Environments from Airborne Chemical, Biological, or Radiological Attacks*, Centers for Disease Control, May 2002 (Pub No. 2002-139).

Explosive Detection Dogs

In a previous section, we discussed the use of explosive detection dogs. For major special events, canines trained to detect bombs are used extensively to sweep protected areas. Some of the best-trained and experienced explosive detection canines are part of the Department of Defense and the Bureau of Alcohol, Tobacco, Firearms, and Explosives. Dogs and handlers from these agencies are sometimes used for national special events supported by federal law enforcement. Generally, the perceived value of explosive detection dogs depends on the extent to which an area can be physically and permanently secured after a sweep.

Explosives Threats

Special event security plans need detailed procedures for dealing with improvised explosive device threats and suspicious packages (which may include unattended items). Most law enforcement and fire/EMS agencies already have such protocols. IED threats directed at special events often occur by telephone; sometimes by mail. Telephone operators involved in the event should receive training on protocols for talking to the caller (e.g., obtain information on exact location of bomb, timing for detonation, record the conversation, pay attention to background noises, etc.) and notifying the designated security plan incident commander. Care must be taken not to turn the incident into a panic situation. The incident should be documented on a special form. The ATF has a bomb threat protocol, checklist, and forms available to law enforcement.[60] The FBI also has extensive bomb mitigation and planning guidelines and checklists available from its Bomb Data Center. FBI and ATF bomb technicians are available to assist in site surveys and the development of IED disposal plans.

As noted earlier, intelligence or investigative support should work with the telephone company to install trap and trace devices on the phone lines. Phone lines should also be equipped with caller ID and recording capabilities.

When a bomb threat is received, the event security commander has two choices to review with the event organizers: (1) evacuate immediately or (2) search and locate the bomb or suspicious package and evacuate after the item is located. If the event is on private property, when the threat is first received, the decision to evacuate is primarily up to the event organizers and their security director, with advice from law enforcement. Most security planners opt for the second approach because many threats are just threats intended to disrupt the event. If bomb threat callers (e.g., disgruntled employees) know that your policy is to evacuate each time a call is made, they can continually call and force events to a standstill.

However, if an explosive device is detected, law enforcement immediately takes over command and decides on the evacuation steps.

The event security commander should follow the incident command system protocol for handling the bomb threat or dealing with the suspicious package. The protocol should have procedures for the following:

- Dispatching a designated bomb disposal unit to the scene of the bomb or package.

- Securing the vicinity around the item and evacuating the area (clear the blast zone).

- Eliminating the threat by examining the item to determine that it is not hazardous, or if hazardous, rendering it safe, or by removing the item from the event area in a safe manner (e.g., using a bomb robot).[61]

[60]See www.atf.gov/press/breakingnews/resources.htm. See *Guidelines from the UK Home Office* at www.mi5.gov.uk/output/Page-11.html.

[61]See www.nlectc.org/techbeat/summer2004/04-Building%20A%20Robot.pdf.

Intelligence

Intelligence information can be very helpful in detecting hazmat materials and WMD. For example, intelligence officers can use resources to obtain information on stolen chemicals and other bomb-making materials, such as large quantities of fertilizer. Fertilizer (ammonium nitrate) is highly explosive when mixed with diesel or fuel oil. This mixture was used in the 1995 Oklahoma City bombing. Intelligence officers or investigators can also seek information on stolen or rented trucks that might be used as vehicle bombs.

The United States Bomb Data Center (USBDC) has standardized the way in which the US Department of Justice captures and shares bomb incident data. ATF shares this information with state and local law enforcement through its Bomb Arson Tracking System.

Emergency Evacuation Plan

A key part of responding to a terrorist incident, bomb attack, or any emergency (e.g., fire) during a major special event is to have a well-designed emergency evacuation plan. The purpose of the evacuation plan is to move spectators and visitors safely and efficiently out of the facility and away from danger or potential injury.

Practically all stadiums, arenas, and other facilities holding special events will have existing emergency evacuation plans that should have been reviewed by the fire department or fire marshal. The main responsibility of the lead security agency is to reexamine those emergency evacuation plans and ensure that they are coordinated into the overall security plan for the event.

The lead security agency should ensure that all officers involved in security of the event receive evacuation plans and that those posted in and around the facility have gone through some level of training on implementing the evacuation plan.

60

Some key issues to consider in developing an emergency evacuation plan for special events include the following:

- Have key security planners and event organizers agreed on criteria for designating an evacuation?

- Is the evacuation plan up-to-date, e.g., taking into account any facility redesign?

- Has the evacuation plan been approved by the fire department, fire marshal, or other city or county inspections office?

- Does the plan designate an overall emergency evacuation coordinator?

- Does the plan show floor plans with marked evacuation routes?

- Are exits clearly marked and designated for evacuation?

- Does the plan include assisting the handicapped?

- Have emergency traffic routes been planned?

- Have specific evacuation attendants or monitors been identified to stand at key locations to provide directions to the exiting crowd?

- Does the facility post or broadcast evacuation messages to spectators prior to an event? The National Football League has developed an emergency evacuation video for stadiums to show on big screens before each game.

- Does the facility conduct periodic emergency evacuation drills?

- Has the lead security agency designated a staging area for law enforcement, fire, EMS, and other assistance?

11. Tactical Support and Crisis Management

Key Questions to Ask:

Do we have local specialized tactical resources (SWAT teams)?

Do the threat and risk levels for the special event require involving the tactical resources?

Have security planners coordinated with the local FBI for crisis management support?

Special events have been inviting targets of opportunity in the past for hostage taking incidents.[62] Depending on the nature of the special event and the perceived threat level (e.g., specific intelligence, DHS raising the threat level from yellow to orange, etc.), security planners should consider engaging support from specialized tactical units, for example, SWAT (special weapons and tactics) teams, to either work the event, be on standby at an off site location, or be on call.

Many city, county, and state law enforcement agencies have SWAT capabilities. These tactical assets often include capabilities such as hostage negotiation, counter assault, counter sniper, counter surveillance, and more.

If SWAT capabilities exist in the jurisdiction, they also include detailed policies, procedures, and protocols covering rules of engagement, tactics, and more. By including SWAT capabilities in the special event security plan, the plan will include the SWAT standard operating procedures (SOPs).

Multiple SWAT units from city, county, and state law enforcement often provide services to jurisdictions in a regional area. These units should be familiar with each other's staffing, equipment, and capabilities. A specialized mutual aid agreement and protocol should be developed for multiple SWAT units that might be employed to provide security at a large special event. These units should come together before the event to plan response and contingencies, and participate in joint training exercises.

For smaller special events, SWAT units may not be present-either on standby, or immediately available. Police security personnel at such events should have training in handling "active shooter" situations. This training instructs police officers in acting as small units to immediately take coordinated tactical action at a shooting in progress. Many police departments have adopted this protocol as a response to school safety issues raised by the Columbine school tragedy.

If any type of terrorist act occurs during a local special event, the FBI is the lead agency in the nation to handle terrorist responses and investigations. The FBI brings a variety of resources to deal with terrorist threats or incidents including well-trained tactical response teams, expert hostage negotiators, forensic investigators, and others.

In the event of a terrorist incident, the law enforcement response would be coordinated by the FBI in accordance with the Terrorism Incident Annex of the National Response Plan. The National Response Plan also outlines the process for requesting assistance from military resources. Another federal specialized resource available for tactical support is the ATF Special Response Team Program, which has teams based in Detroit, Los Angeles, Dallas, and Washington, D.C., available to respond anywhere in the U.S. to conduct high-risk law enforcement operations.

[62] In the 1972 Munich Olympics, PLO terrorists took Israeli athletes hostages in an attempt to obtain freedom for Arab prisoners—11 athletes were ultimately killed. This was a turning point for special events security.

12. Public Information and Media Relations

Key Questions to Ask:

Have we developed an adequate public information and media relations plan as part of our event security operations plan?

Have we identified the event public information specialist who will coordinate all public and media information?

If the event involves planned demonstrations, have event organizers, government officials, and law enforcement developed a consistent message regarding demonstration activities?

Special events involve an extensive amount of information that needs to be communicated to partner agencies, other surrounding governments, potential event spectators or attendees, businesses and the community, and the media. Key decisions for security planners are to identify the lead coordinator for public information and the process for releasing information. The DHS has developed a useful guide as part of the National Response Plan (see, Public Affairs Support Annex, pg. 289).[63]

The public information specialist should be closely involved in all stages of a special event: pre-event planning, event implementation and management, post-event activities, and especially if any major incidents occur. The public information specialist should assist in developing a public information and media relations plan for the special event. During the event, public information office staff should also be in the central command center.

There are two types of public information related to special events. One involves general information about the event—when the entrance doors or gates are open, when certain performers or activities begin and end, which VIPs are attending, parking locations, and more. The other involves security—what items are allowed (and not allowed) into the event, how to evacuate in case of emergency, where first aid services are located, and the like.

The lead law enforcement agency and event organizers need to collaborate closely to decide what information will be released and who will release it. One option is to have the city or county public information officer or, if the event is private, the private agency's media relations specialist, handle all information dissemination, press conferences, and more. This would include security-related information that has been approved for release by the lead law enforcement agency. The other option is for the city or county PIO to defer security-related matters to the lead law enforcement agency.

If the event has commercial considerations, as many special events do, the public information staff needs to meet with the event's marketing staff to ensure a consistent message for information to the public and media about the event. For example, what is the image of the event? What is newsworthy about the event? How does the event benefit the community? What VIPs will be making appearances at the event?

An important aspect of special event security public relations is to involve citizens and the business community in security planning for the event when they will be affected by the event. When the security plan calls for closing roads or sidewalks that will reduce car and pedestrian traffic and shoppers from using certain businesses, the event organizers along with law enforcement should meet with the affected businesses early in the planning process to discuss the security plans and determine if any accommodations can be made so that the businesses will not suffer a negative economic impact from the event.

Additionally, citizens need to know if their normal commuting routes and transportation modes will be altered during the special event.

If a special event involves planned protests and demonstrations, law enforcement needs to work with city or county officials and event organizers to develop and disseminate a clear and consistent message on how demonstrations will be handled. As noted earlier in Section 2 on communications, Savannah-Chatham Police Chief Dan Flynn recounts that when he was preparing security for the 2004 G-8 Summit in Sea Island, Georgia, he learned from the Mayor of Calgary, which had hosted the June 2003 World Trade Organization Summit, to develop and stress a clear and consistent message to all

[63]See www.dhs.gov/
interweb/assetlibrary/NRP
FullText.pdf.

potential event participants—and encourage all key players to always stay on point. Thus, the media message for the G-8 in Georgia, and the WTO event later in Miami, was that participants (and demonstrators) can come to Savannah and express their First Amendment views, but if they break the law in any way, they will be swiftly and effectively arrested and prosecuted.

In terms of public relations, the NYPD, in preparing for the 2004 Republican National Convention, developed a pocket-sized (7½ x 4 inches) publication entitled *Officers' Guide to the Republican National Convention*. This 48-page handbook was distributed to all officers who worked in the field during the convention. The handbook contained information helpful to the public such as important telephone numbers and addresses (e.g., city agencies; federal agencies; police precincts; hospitals; sporting events; places of interest—zoo, museums, stores; Broadway theaters; hotels) and maps. The booklet also provided tips to officers on:

- Signs of possible terrorist activity

- Officer appearance and demeanor—"demonstrate courtesy, professionalism, and respect"

- Mandatory equipment

- Cooperation with news media

- Police conduct at demonstrations

- Street closures

13. Training

Specialized training is a common preparation activity for law enforcement in the pre-event security planning stages for major special events. In all the special event after-action reports reviewed by the study team, no agency ever said that it had received too much training prior to an event; although many said that they wished they could have received more.

Early in the event security planning stage, one of the important tasks of the major special event training team or subcommittee is to conduct a training needs assessment with the other planning teams—what specialized knowledge and skills are needed to effectively implement the security plan? By identifying the broad range of specialized knowledge and skills needed in the security plan and then comparing that to the planned workforce, the lead security agency can determine the type and level of training that is needed.

For the most part, professional law enforcement agencies can rely on specialized support units to train routinely. For example, the personnel that are part of SWAT, bomb detection (dogs) and disposal units, traffic escort/motorcade squads, and others train regularly to maintain their skills. In planning to use them as support units for the specialized event, they just need to adapt their skills and knowledge to the security plan. These units do not have to be specially trained for the special event.

Most of the specialized training should be directed toward communicating and cooperating effectively among the various agencies (law enforcement, fire/EMS, others) that will be working together on the event. Other training needs to be directed to field forces when events include the threat of disruptions from protestors.

Private security forces managing special events also need specialized training. For example, in the National Football League's Best Practices for Security, the following direction is provided to stadium managers:

> Conduct at least one annual emergency drill prior to or early in the season. During training scenarios, test the chain of command, decision making process, primary/secondary communications and emergency use of the PA and video systems.[64]

Training Topics

Survey results showed a variety of training topics delivered in preparing personnel for special events; however, the following stand out as the most common:

- Incident command system (ICS)/Unified command (UC). Because of the multi-agency nature of the security plan for major special events, most lead agencies find it advisable to deliver this training to the command staff of the various agencies, especially those who will be in the communications command center during the special event.

- Use of specialized equipment. In events where new equipment for communications, security (e.g., magnetometers; video cameras), or other areas is purchased, it is advisable to provide training to the people who will operate and use the equipment. For example, for the recent Republican National Convention, the NYPD trained officers to operate new scooters, bicycles, and vehicle checkpoint equipment.

- Orientation to security plan for the Special Event. All personnel should be briefed and trained to some degree on the security plan for the particular special event.

- Legal issues. Providing key command staff and field supervisors with refresher training on legal issues that may come up during security operations for the event (e.g., search and seizure, use of force, arrests, etc.) is advisable.

- Crowd control. Where the special event includes the threat of disruption from demonstrators, the entire field force must receive training in crowd control tactics, use of force (rules of engagement), and more.

- Use of personal protective equipment. If officers have not already received personal protective equipment (masks, gloves, etc.) training for use in case of a chemical or biological threat, it should be delivered prior to the event.

- Recognizing signs of possible terrorist activities. For special events since 9/11, many law enforcement agencies are delivering training to all security field forces in recognizing signs of possible terrorist activities (e.g., unusual bulges in clothing, attempts to avoid law enforcement personnel, clothing that is unsuitable for the season, ATF training on IEDs and unattended packages, etc.).

[64] See National Football League, *Best Practices for Stadium Security*, 2002.

In preparing for the G-8 Summit in Georgia, the Georgia Bureau of Investigations required the thousands of law enforcement personnel assigned to security to take at least eight hours of training classes covering such topics as rights of protestors, use of less-then-lethal weapons, venue security, and terrorism tactics. They also delivered practical hands-on exercises on using equipment (riot gear), performing surveillance, operating in teams, and more.

Several departments surveyed (e.g., Austin, Denver, Portland, Virginia Beach) discussed past events where civil disturbances had broken out. Subsequently, they have incorporated lessons learned into their department's crowd control training and adjusted their strategies for deploying tactical units at special events.

Methods of Training Delivery

There are obviously many methods for delivering special event security training. Jurisdictions that are responsible for handling large special events annually may want to consider building event security planning and management into their local/regional training academy. Some of the more common training methods obtained in reviews of how law enforcement is handling event security include the following:

- Roll call training. This is useful to deliver brief subjects or a series of subjects over several days. Departments have used this mainly to provide an overview on the security plan prior to the event on general subjects such as courtesy and demeanor during the event.

- Video training. This is useful when time is limited and officers can be given videos to watch at home. For the Republican National Convention, the NYPD prepared six training videos covering crowd control, working at train stations, recognizing suspected terrorist activities, legal issues, and more.

- Handouts. This is another method to reach a lot of personnel quickly and easily. Departments often use this form for fairly self-explanatory material such as road closings, post locations, etc. This allows officers to review the materials at a convenient time.

- Web site. Materials, articles, reports, and written procedures (e.g., prisoner processing) can also be posted on the department's web site for officers to review and download.

- Tabletop exercises. This is essential for security of events that involve multiple agencies. This allows command staff representing each agency to walk through a variety of scenarios that could happen at the event. It allows the agencies to review and test existing procedures and plans; make adjustments; clarify command, control, and communications protocols; and identify deficiencies or duplications of effort. This training also helps build relationships, trust, and a commitment to the security plan among participants.

- Field exercises. This allows agencies to walk through realistic scenarios in the field. It is especially useful for crowd control training.

The Phoenix Police Department, for example, has conducted a number of live training events as well as tabletop exercises in preparing for special events. These include a 2004 tabletop biohazard training event that included various state agencies and focused on whether to evacuate and the safest evacuation plan for different hazards and different venues (baseball stadium, basketball arena, etc.). Phoenix completed one full-blown disaster exercise (pre-9/11) where the scenario involved terrorists entering a ballpark, releasing a toxic substance, and shooting at random. This exercise included 200 volunteers from the ballpark posing as victims. Another mock disaster exercise was conducted at the airport over eight hours (only Phoenix personnel participated). In this scenario, a bomb released a toxic chemical while a plane was taxiing. The staging area was an executive taxiing area located about 200 yards from other planes and runways, and 100 volunteers participated as passengers. These exercises were considered very productive, but the costs can be significant. For example, for the ballpark exercise, the cost for Phoenix participants alone (on-duty and overtime salaries for Phoenix police, fire, and EMS personnel but excluding sheriff's department and ballpark personnel) was approximately $50,000.

Training Considerations

Some important training considerations were suggested by law enforcement agencies in the national surveys of law enforcement special event security practices. A few of the most significant training considerations are listed below:

- Train more officers than needed. NYPD trained 480 officers to use new scooters but used only 300 during the RNC.

- Begin to deliver training early in the planning process. This allows agencies to save time for last minute remedial training.

- Maintain a comprehensive log of who received which type of training (officer's name, agency, training, etc.) for the event. This information may become important in later legal issues.

- Obtain feedback on training. Include feedback on training usefulness in the after-action report.

Training During the Event

If security at a special event lasts for several days, like the Olympics, agencies might consider doing some exercises during the event to help maintain officers' focus (on what could happen) and attention to detail. Sometimes boredom sets in due to the routine nature of security. This is a recommendation from the report on security at the Salt Lake City Olympics (Greene, 2002).

Training Resources

Some of the most useful resources for training to prepare to plan and manage major special events include the federal agencies that are involved in securing large special events: Secret Service, FBI, ATF, and FEMA. FEMA's Emergency Management Institute[65] has courses related to ICS for Law Enforcement, and Special Events Contingency Planning for Public Safety Agencies. The private sector also has capabilities to deliver training in event security.

In 2005, some of the COPS Office's Regional Community Policing Institutes will be offering a training course on planning and managing security for major special events.[66]

[65] See http://training.fema. gov/EMIWeb/EMICourses.

[64] See www.cops.usdoj. gov/Default.asp?Item=115 or call the COPS Office Response Center at 800.421.6770.

14. Planning for and Managing Demonstrations

Key Questions to Ask:

Have we received useful intelligence information to advise the security plan on anticipated protest movements at the event?

Do we have adequate support from police legal advisors?

Do we have sufficient numbers of trained mobile field forces to make mass arrests if necessary?

Have we issued rules of engagement to all field forces involved in event security?

One of the most contentious and potentially dangerous issues affecting the security of major special events, besides possible terrorist attacks, is disruptive and unlawful behavior by protestors or celebratory behavior. Protestors often come to special events, such as World Trade Organizations meetings, political gatherings (inaugurations, memorials, meetings with foreign heads of state), and other social or cultural events, to disrupt the events, obtain media attention to causes, embarrass governments and law enforcement, and to damage property.

Law enforcement, on the other hand, must draw a difficult balance between protecting the First Amendment and other civil rights of the lawful protestors while maintaining the safe and secure continuation of the event.

In this guidelines report, discussion of law enforcement managing civil disturbances and crowd control at special events is limited. There are a variety of other resources that cover this topic in much more depth.[67]

Protestor Tactics

Protestors and law enforcement officials have been interconnected throughout the world for centuries. In the U.S., many state police organizations were started by legislatures to control demonstrators who were protesting labor conditions at mines and factories. Law enforcement in the U.S. faced decades of civil disturbances over civil rights and the war in Vietnam in the 1960s and 70s. In the past five years, police have had to deal more with neo-eclectic protest movements related to environmental conditions, world trade, animal rights, self-proclaimed "anarchists," and more. In addition, some of the protestors have become more organized (using the Internet) and more violent.

Some of the tactics listed below have been assembled by reviewing police departments after-action reports of special events that included attempted disruptive behavior by protest groups.

In addition, police are facing more "celebratory riots" related to sporting events. An Iowa State University working group exploring the causes of a recent student riot and the police response issued a report entitled, Factors Contributing to and Dynamics of Iowa State University Campus Disturbances.[68] In this report, the university working group noted the following:

> The riot that took place in Ames in the early morning of Sunday, April 18, 2004, is part of a nationwide wave of campus disturbances arising from a variety of situations. Since 1985, there have been over 200 of these disturbances, and their frequency is increasing. These mixed-issue disturbances, like the April 18 riot, are distinguished from previous campus riots in that they are not clearly connected to protest. Sometimes called "celebratory riots," they are often marked by a mood of celebration.

Many of these student riots have involved celebrations around sporting events.

[67]See Report by the Special Advisor to the Board of Police Commissioners on the Civil Disorder in Los Angeles, *The City in Crisis,* October 1992; Police Foundation, *What Do We Know? How Should We Prepare?* 1994.

[68]Working Group, Iowa State University, *Factors Contributing to and Dynamics of Iowa State University Campus Disturbances,* see www.iastate.edu/news/04/veishea/meetings/tf/group2finalreport.pdf.

Some of the common protestor tactics have included the following:

- Stealing security fencing and erecting it to block streets

- Setting fires in the street

- Chaining themselves to objects (sewer grates, light poles) and each other to make it difficult to arrest them

- Locking their arms into concrete sleeves ('sleeping dragons') to make it difficult for police to place handcuffs on their wrists

- Moving dumpsters in the street or rolling them toward officers

- Bringing other large objects into the street (large blocks of concrete from a construction site)

- Trying to 'lockdown' an intersection by lying down in the street

- Erecting platforms and stages in the street

- Putting chains across an intersection—light pole to light pole

- Trying to disable police vehicles by flattening the tires

- Using chemical irritants against the police

- Throwing rocks, bottles, and other missiles at the police

- Riding bicycles to lookout and report on police forces locations and tactics

- Using a mass of bicycles to block street traffic

- Communicating with each other by cell phone (point-to-point)

- Wearing gas masks, bandannas, and protective equipment to block the effect of chemical irritants

- Using a variety of 'baiting' tactics including shouting insults, passive resistance, and videotaping officers.

Legal Support

In developing security plans, training, and response tactics to deal with protestors, legal advice is essential. Police attorneys or city or county attorneys are also involved early in the event planning process to negotiate on behalf of the police department and city or county with groups seeking permits to march or assemble and demonstrate during the event. Early in the planning process for the Republican National Convention, the NYPD attorneys met with dozens of groups and associations to review and negotiate assembly permits. The Boston Police Department's attorneys started negotiating with the ACLU and other groups 18 months before the Democratic National Convention.

Legal support is also helpful to provide training and procedural tips for dealing with protestor activities. Legal advice to refresh the issues and place them in context is useful especially regarding use of force (rules of engagement), detention of persons, searches, seizures of property, and arrests. For the RNC, the NYPD legal staff produced a useful 36-page handbook entitled Legal Guidelines for the Republican National Convention. The handbook includes an overview of First Amendment rights, general types of protestor conduct and tactics, processing arrests, common charges, penal code sections, and more.

During the arrest processing stage, it is also helpful to have prosecutors or police attorneys present to debrief arresting officers and review charges and evidence.

Restricting Access

One of the preferred methods of managing protest groups at special events is to create protest zones and restrict the access and movement of groups—keeping them safely away from secure areas that are being used by VIPs, political figures, and other event attendees. In recent years of special events, especially those with political figures or foreign dignitaries or heads of state, law enforcement has used barriers effectively to wall off demonstrators from the objects of their demonstrations.

At the 2004 Democratic National Convention in Boston, the police created a designated demonstration zone that allowed protestors to be within "sight and sound" of the convention delegates (close to the parking lot where the delegates got off buses to enter the Fleet Center) but provided enough protection (jersey barriers with fencing, wire mesh, etc.) to effectively keep the demonstrators from physically threatening the delegates. The ACLU, filing suit on behalf of one group, claimed that the "demonstrator pens" violated freedom of expression guaranteed by the First Amendment to the Constitution.

The U.S. Court of Appeals, calling this a very close case, noted the balance in rights. "On the one hand, freedom of expression, especially freedom of political expression, is vital to the health of our democracy. On the other hand, making public safety a reality and ensuring that important political events are able to proceed normally are also valuable." The Court went on to uphold the District Court ruling that the security measures, "though extreme," were nonetheless narrowly tailored and did not deny freedom of speech.[69]

Crowd Management Response

[69] Black Tea Society v. City of Boston, U.S. Court of Appeals for the First Circuit, No. 04-2002, July 30, 2004.

Local police surveyed for this report varied in how (or whether) they deployed special crowd management response units. The key factors in even deploying the units were the nature of the event and the extent of the threat from protestors or possibility of celebratory disturbances. Often, they discussed crowd management in terms of taking a "soft approach at first." That is, the department did not use mobile force units as a matter of routine. Instead, crowd control officers with distinct uniforms and riot gear would be positioned in the background or were not even visible but were on duty, close by, and ready to act quickly if called upon.

In special events with obvious and stated protest movements by extremist groups or "anarchists"[70] who have a history of attempting to disrupt events and destroying property, law enforcement must be ready with sizeable and trained field forces capable of countering any attempts to disrupt planned events, destroy property, or break the law. In these situations, law enforcement must be prepared for mass arrest situations.

One of the most effective law enforcement responses to quell disruptive protest disturbances appears to be the deployment of a variety of mobile field forces or strike teams. These are teams of officers, equipped with crowd control gear (helmets with visors, batons, chemical irritants, possibly shields, and more), which may include smaller teams (8-10) and larger teams (40-50). Some of the teams, in order to be highly mobile in congested areas, may ride scooters or bicycles. The NYPD deployed teams on both types of vehicles for the recent RNC.

These mobile field teams are not to be confused with SWAT teams. The mobile field teams are typically trained patrol officers, not SWAT officers. SWAT officers may also be deployed at the event (see discussion under Section 11, Tactical Support and Crisis Management) but in a tactical support capacity. However, some special events commanders advocate also using SWAT as mobile field teams because they might otherwise just remain in reserve for the entire event.

Tracking the movement and placement of mobile field forces is critical to their effective use in controlling crowds. In the 1999 Seattle WTO event, some field forces became cut off from support teams because radio communication was not always functional. The quality and effectiveness of radio communication (discussed in Section 2) between the field forces and the central communications command post is essential. At the recent G-8 Summit event in Georgia, some field supervisors were equipped with GPS tracking chips in their cell phones that were connected to mapping software in the command center. Thus, the exact movement of the teams could be observed on computer maps.

In crowd control situations during special events, security forces must be ever mindful about controlling use of force by officers. In events involving multiple security agencies, the lead agency must take the lead and develop some common rules of engagement for all the other agencies to agree to abide by (this agreement should be in writing) during the event. During the G-8 Summit event, the Savannah-Chatham Police Department's standard use of force continuum process was streamlined to be easier to understand in the field. The following illustrations were provided:

- Officer Presence: Uniformed police presence. This presence may be in platoon formation. There is no physical contact between police and the demonstrators.

- Physical Force: The force involving hands-on touching, to include riot baton, asp, and protective riot shield. There is no deployment of chemical weapons. This tactic may include line and wedge formations to move the crowd. Arrests may also fall into this category.

- Chemical Force: The use of weapons that disperse chemical irritants. Chemical force includes the use of OC spray, both hand-held and MK-46 canisters, and CS agents (tear gas).

- Deadly Force: "Deadly Force" is defined as that force which is intended to cause death or grave injury or which creates some specific degree of risk that a reasonable and prudent person would consider likely to cause death or grave injury.

The event rules of engagement also went on to define deadly force. Use of force must always be controlled, but especially during civil disturbances. Improper force can create new issues for extremist groups, the public, and the media to attack. Force applied to the wrong parties cannot be justified. It is particularly important that use of force policies be understood and complied with by all police personnel. Two key issues during civil disturbances are deadly force and OC/chemical agents. It is recommended that the following guidelines serve as the basic framework for the explanation of departmental policy in this area:

- Deadly force will be used only to protect lives in immediate danger.

- Deadly force will not be directed at offenders involved in property crimes if lives are not in immediate danger.

- Force of any type will be used only to the legal extent required to control a given situation.

- The use of OC/chemical agents will be strictly controlled by the on-scene commander.

In order to maintain accountability, the Savannah-Chatham Police Department coded all chemical agent canisters that were distributed to all officers. Thus, when an expended canister was recovered it could be linked to the officer who discharged it.

Law enforcement must continuously evaluate the use of less lethal weapons in crowd control situations. Use of OC pepper spray by police to break up a fight in the stands at a 2003 Monday Night NFL game caused a contamination problem—the spray extended to the electric fans on the field and spread to the players' bench on the field, causing several players to become momentarily ill; the game was stopped for about ten minutes. This particular police agency now allows officers to use only OC foam in the stadium.

Some departments also document how field forces handle crowd situations by videotaping events in the field. The Philadelphia Police Department has its video unit do this as a matter of routine. They find that it helps with after-action reports.

[70] The 'anarchists' movement, e.g., www.greenanarchy.org, appears to have a number of self-proclaimed members who loosely adhere to a variety of anti-government rhetoric but have admittedly been involved in demonstrations involving property destruction.

Tips for Officer Conduct at Demonstrations*

- Remain calm. Don't overreact. Never let your guard down.

- Be aware of the media. Anyone in the crowd could have a cell phone camera and instantly beam video to the Internet.

- Be tactful and patient when directing people to move.

- Work as a team, not as an individual.

- Treat everyone with courtesy, professionalism, and respect.

- Refer all civilian complaints to the citizens' complaint number.

- Take action only in coordination with the field supervisors and field commanders—don't act alone.

* Many of these were adapted from the NYPD's *Officers' Guide to the Republican National Convention*

Community Policing and Demonstration Management

The city of Portland, Oregon, which has its share of protest movements, also has a strong community policing history. The police department emphasizes a community policing approach for negotiating with protesters and, as a result, preventing disruptions. The event commander seeks out and initiates meetings with protest organizers who apply for march permits or are otherwise known to police—such as representatives of unions or police accountability groups—and with others who are not yet known, such as anarchists. In August 2003, Portland police successfully employed a community policing approach to aid in managing protesters whose leadership appeared to be anarchist. The site was a park, which was near a University of Portland facility that was being visited by the President of the United States. A total of about 3,000 people assembled in the park for this event.

The anarchists did not obtain a march permit but, a few days before the event, they did send a liaison to meet with the police department's liaison to the crowd. At the meeting, the police discussed the "rules of engagement," determined what most wanted (media coverage and a good viewing area), and suspected that there might be other elements in the crowd who would be interested in more aggressive outcomes, like breaching barricades and stopping the motorcade. Police made decisions that gave the larger, less threatening group most of what it wanted. This separated out the more dangerous group, and the police were able to control it.

Intelligence

As noted earlier in the discussion about the role of intelligence supporting event security (Section 5), intelligence support is essential in preparing security plans for an event involving potentially disruptive groups. Proactive intelligence can provide information to security planners in the planning stages such as crowd estimates, history of prior tactics at other events, criminal histories of known individuals, and more.

Pre-event intelligence information can be obtained by interviewing police from jurisdictions that had events where these groups participated, by monitoring web sites used by the groups, and even interviewing some of the group leaders (see Portland example above).

During the event, intelligence information can be obtained by inserting intelligence officers into group meetings and monitoring the activities of the groups. Meetings can also be held with group leaders.

Cooperation with Private Security

Salt Lake City regularly handles groups that protest at the semi-annual conventions of the Church of Jesus Christ of Latter-day Saints (LDS). Protesters assemble to convey messages about religious beliefs, animal rights, gay rights, and other issues. Although the LDS Church has not taken a position on the Iraq war, anti-war protesters also gather. Temple Square is the property of the LDS Church, and convention events are ticketed (no public admission). However, anyone can come into the Temple Square area as long as they abide by certain rules (no smoking, no drinking, etc.). The Tabernacle seats 4,500-5,000; the Temple seats 22,000; and 50,000-60,000 people a day gather on the lawns and grounds during the conventions. Salt Lake City police explain that the keys to successfully managing these events are to (1) staff the event adequately to effectively handle protests and (2) to obtain and share intelligence ahead of time on who is expected to be there protesting. The police department and the LDS Church exchange information about threats as part of planning. The LDS Church has its own Security Department responsible for security of the buildings and assets. The LDS Church also has its own explosive detection canines, dozens of video cameras, and high-tech equipment in its command center. Since 9/11, the police department reports that the LDS Church began using magnetometers at the entries to the buildings.

Joint Training with Multiple Agencies

As mentioned above, the Iowa State University working group exploring the causes of a recent student riot and the police response issued a report that recommended, among other areas, that police departments in university communities that respond together to handle student riots should engage in "multijurisdictional training, coordination and planning" to prepare for such disturbances. [71]

Mass Arrest Plan

In special events involving protestors intent on disrupting the event and breaking the law, law enforcement must have sufficient forces to make mass arrests to foil disruptive protestors who are intent on shutting down lawful movement of traffic and pedestrians or city functions. The Seattle Police Department did not have enough forces at the 1999 WTO meeting. Though they made over 600 arrests over several days, they did not have enough back up to arrest all the lawbreakers on the spot. In contrast, during the RNC, the NYPD had many more forces and made over 1,800 arrests quickly quelling disruptive and unlawful protestor behavior.

For example, in one afternoon, several thousand bicyclists intended to shut down traffic at several major intersections of the downtown area near the convention center. The NYPD responded to this threat with mobile field forces on foot, bicycles, and scooters. They arrested over 300 demonstrators and seized their bicycles (though it was a challenge to transport and store the bikes).

The mass arrest plan for disruptive protestors at special events is dependent on sufficient officer forces and an efficient arrest-processing plan. The specialized prisoner processing procedures developed for the special event should be distributed to all field forces, used for training at roll calls prior to the event, and possibly put on videotape and distributed to all partner agencies.

As an alternative to arresting disruptive individuals who have destroyed public or private property during a special event, some police agencies videotape the demonstrators and try to identify them later. Some university police agencies have started to do this at celebratory riots. Some campus security agencies also post photos of unidentified violators on the Internet requesting that other students identify them.

Some consideration in mass arrest planning include the following:

- Do we have adequate numbers of trained staff to make mass arrests in the field?

- Have we distributed enough equipment (flex cuffs, etc.)?

- Do we have adequate numbers of vehicles to transport the prisoners from the scene?

- Do we have adequate space and staff at the processing/booking facility?

- Do we have prosecutors or police attorneys at the booking facility to review charges with officers?

- Are detention facilities adequate, safe, and clean?

- If prisoners stay longer than a few hours, do we have adequate food, water/beverages, and restrooms?

- Can we segregate prisoner types from each other—male/female, adult/juvenile, etc.?

- Do we have facilities to decontaminate prisoners exposed to chemical agents?

- Do we have adequate screening to take injured prisoners for medical care? Handle prisoners with disabilities?

- Can prisoners receive speedy court appearances/judicial review of charges?

Miscellaneous Event-Related Control Laws and Issues

In our surveys of local law enforcement, some additional crowd control laws and issues were raised. A few examples:

- Alcohol Violations. Several local departments surveyed for this report explained that prohibiting alcohol sales and consumption at various special events has been key to achieving security and safety goals. The "noalcohol" events tend to attract a more family-oriented crowd, resulting in fewer fights and other incidents. Several other departments reported that strict alcohol enforcement has improved safety at events where alcohol is sold or permitted—including cooler checks, underage buys, and a reputation for low tolerance of alcohol-related activity.

- Juvenile Curfew Laws. Jurisdictions must consider the extent to which police will enforce juvenile curfew laws and—if they decide on strict enforcement—provide the extra resources needed to handle curfew violators. The Austin (Texas) Police Department has made a concerted effort for Mardi Gras to deal with juvenile curfew violators (10:00 p.m. for ages 16 and under). In the past, special busses have been arranged to transport youth out of the festival area, and police have called parents/guardians to pick them up. However, attention to enforcing the juvenile curfew law is often limited because most of the available police resources must be devoted to crowd control.

- Lost Children. An important part of planning for events that attract families—July 4th celebrations, festivals, state fairs, etc.—includes procedures for handling lost children. One security commander pointed out that events like state fairs attract their share of pedophiles, not just pickpockets and petty thieves. The Tulsa County (Oklahoma) Sheriff's Office devotes a great deal of thought and planning to preventing lost child situations and taking care of found children until parents/guardians are located. The department sets up a trailer at an entrance to issue identification (armbands) for children. At the last fair, about 20,000 were given out. In addition, members of the chaplain's program are stationed there to entertain and comfort lost children until their parents are found.

- Gangs. Several jurisdictions discussed gang-related problems associated with various events. For example, the San Diego County Sheriff's Department notes a historical problem with "turf wars" on the first day of the San Diego County Fair in mid-June. In 2003, intelligence about a retaliatory gang shooting prompted overnight installation of metal detectors. In addition to assessing intelligence about potential gang threats, several departments discussed pro-active measures taken during or immediately before special events to identify gang members or gang-related activity. In one city, bus drivers notify police of potential gang members they observe among passengers being transported to large events. Undercover officers meet the bus and follow the suspects.

Security Management During the Event

Security management during the special event means overseeing the implementation of the security plan. This phase begins as spectators, officials, crowds, media, and others begin to assemble at the event site. For some events, Super Bowl, NASCAR races, conventions, people begin to gather days prior to the actual event or game.

This phase includes comprehensive communications, monitoring, and reporting. It involves ensuring that key operational areas are functioning properly, such as the communications command center, credentialing, access control posts, and more. It also involves checking on the readiness of field and support areas such as mobile field forces to deal with crowd control, intelligence support, arrest processing, EMS/medical support, and more.

General Overview—Ensure Readiness

As one special event security manager put it, "This is where the rubber meets the road." The overall special event security director and staff need to ensure that all the personnel, equipment, and other resources are in place and ready to implement the security plan. Useful checklists can help the security directors accomplish this comprehensive set of detailed plans. Some of examples of lists and immediate "To Do" items are shown on the following page.

After ensuring the readiness of all security personnel, including private security, contract guards, volunteers, and others, the security director should meet with the event organizers to be briefed on any last minute changes to the event schedule (e.g., VIPs cancellations, additions, etc.), which are common in special events. Any significant changes to the event agenda should be passed on to the communications command center and then to all key event security supervisors.

At this point, when the event is underway, the security director should engage in "management by walking around." If the central communications command center is located in the main event facility with a view of the event, the security director can spend some time in that location monitoring security. If the central communications command center is off site, then the security director should be represented by his or her next in command at that facility.

Illustrations of Event Security Management Checklists/'To Do' Lists

- List of contact information (cell phone, pager, radio call sign, PDA, etc.) for main contacts (on-scene commanders, supervisors, etc.) of all other cooperating/involved agencies. This should be in alphabetical order by name.

- Same list of key contact information but ordered by type of assignment or post (e.g., supervisor on Access Gate A, supervisor in charge of SWAT team, etc.)

- List of contacts for key outside agencies that may be called in for support if not already involved in security of event, e.g., FBI, ATF, FEMA, state transportation agency, etc.

- Annotated summaries of security operational plan (full plan accessible)

- Annotated agenda of event—what happens when and where—with key security notes added in

- Maps and geographic layouts showing codes for response locations, e.g., Gate A, Blue parking lot, etc.

- Contact all supervisors to determine if all personnel have checked in

- Check with all resources that have been placed on alert and on-call status—e.g., K-9 team—bomb dog, bomb experts, helicopter access, etc.

Final Security Briefing

Final security briefings are essential for communicating key points in the event security plan and any last minute changes. These briefings are typically held early in the morning several hours before the event begins. Ideally, if time and logistics permit, and depending on the size and complexity of the event, it is useful to brief all personnel involved in implementing the security plan at the same time (may need a large space like a gymnasium or auditorium). Where the event is too large and involves too many security personnel, the briefing may be limited to command staff and supervisors.

If the event takes place over several days and involves officers on different shifts, additional briefings should be held at the beginning of each shift change.

When events involve protestors, it is always best for the lead agency to make sure that the rules of engagement have been clearly and consistently explained to all field officers, especially those from outside agencies. Miscommunication can sometimes occur when a supervisor from an outside agency hears the briefing and then later tries to communicate it to his or her officers. Some of the key points typically covered in final security briefings include those listed below.

Examples of key points to cover and procedures to review in final security briefings include the following:

- Ensure that commanders, supervisors, and key officers have contact lists, maps, and annotated event agendas
- Remind everyone to check all equipment—especially radios (ping communications center; know call signs); report any malfunctions immediately
- Last minute intelligence reports
- Logistics support plans—when personnel will have breaks, food and drinks, receive necessary supplies, etc.
- After-action recommendations from previous event
- Specific key assignments
- Communications/radio protocol
- Procedure for reporting incidents—minor, major—how response will be handled
- Procedures for dealing with suspicious packages and bomb threats
- Person and vehicle search procedures
- Rules of engagement
- Evacuation procedures.

Field Supervision

During special events, the security director needs to especially monitor all field activities, which is the line of defense where people intent on defeating security will come in contact with security forces. The most important personnel in ensuring the implementation fidelity for the security plan are the field commanders and supervisors. Selecting highly competent, experienced, and professional field commanders and supervisors is the key to implementing event security plans. The security director needs to maintain constant contact with these commanders and supervisors throughout the event to check and monitor security.

Field supervisors should be encouraged to make decisions regarding security issues and problems, in line with the overall operational security plans, at their level. If the problems require management review, supervisors can contact field commanders. Commanders then decide whether the decision is within their scope of authority or refer the decision to the security director. Even if the issue or problem is resolved at lower levels, supervisors and commanders should still notify the central communications command center so that the matter can be recorded. For some key actions (e.g., confrontational situations, any use of force, arrests, injuries to officers, etc.), the security director needs to be notified immediately. The protocol for how and to whom all these issues are communicated should be spelled out in the security operational plan.

Access Control

This is a key part of the security plan that has to be monitored closely during the initial stages of the event for any problems or issues. Is the equipment working properly? Is staff screening carefully enough but also quickly enough—are long lines growing? Are screeners finding anything unusual— weapons, contraband, etc.? Is credentialing review working as planned?

If long lines are starting to build or if other problems are occurring at screening points, the event organizers will likely want the security director to make some adjustments or implement some alternatives to make screening more efficient. Alternatives should be in the operational plan.

Crowd Control

This is another key part of the security plan that has to be monitored very carefully by the security director. If demonstrators are expected at the event, or if law enforcement anticipates celebratory disturbances after the event, the actions of law enforcement will be carefully reviewed and second-guessed by the spectators, media, event organizers, governing officials, and others. There will be extensive pressure on law enforcement to execute this part of the security operational plan properly (see Section 14, Planning for and Managing Demonstrations).

Ground Rules for Problem Behavior

Law enforcement, private security, and event organizers must also agree on what criteria to use for dealing with problem event participants or spectators. In general, as behavior warrants in dealing with problem individuals, the phases of imposing security intervention should include warnings, ejection, and arrest.

The list below represents common behavior problems that range from situations where private security should provide an initial warning to cease the behavior, to ejecting the person from the event, to having law enforcement arrest the person for an illegal act.

Common spectator behavior problems at special events include:

- Blocking aisles, doorways, and emergency exits

- Continual failure to take their seat as ticketed and/or moving to seats not assigned without permission

- Making video or audio recordings without authorization

- Repeated refusal to cooperate with security requests

- Unsafe, uncontrolled, and/or rowdy behavior making it unsafe or disturbing for others

- Entering without a ticket or credential

- Immoral or vulgar behavior

- Stealing

- Ticket scalping

- Fighting

- Intentional property damage

- Alcohol intoxication with unsafe behavior

- Illegal drug use.

Central Communications Command Center

During the event, the security director must ensure that all key agency representatives have shown up and are at their stations in the command post. If someone hasn't shown up, a back-up should be called in. This is especially the case for technicians— internal information technology specialists who helped wire the room and external telecommunications service providers.

Back-up and alternate communications systems should also be checked to ensure readiness. In many major special events, in addition to the central communications command center, there might be additional communications centers that are being operated by some of the participating agencies. For example, during the 2004 Democratic National Convention, while the Secret Service operated the Multi-Agency Command Center (MACC), the Boston Police Department operated its own communications command center (while also participating in the MACC).

Intelligence

One of the critical parts of managing the operational security event is to continue on with a proactive intelligence function. As discussed in Section 5 on intelligence, obtaining and sharing timely information is critical, especially information that could impact event security. Intelligence units should continue to contact sources during the event and provide regular briefings to staff in the central communications command center.

For larger events, intelligence units may also be posted in the field observing event activities, spectators, and others and providing counter surveillance if needed.

Public Information

The role of developing and disseminating coordinated and consistent information becomes very important during major special events. For these events, many media representatives will be attending the event, clamoring for stories to report. The security director needs to work with the designated public information specialist to provide details of newsworthy incidents that do not hamper security (or possible future investigations and prosecution, depending on the nature of the incident).

Post-Event Activities

After a special event is completed, the security operations director needs to oversee the process of finalizing the logistics wrap-up, completing accounting activities, and preparing an after-action report. Each of these important processes will be discussed on the next page.

Logistics Wrap-Up

Event security personnel assigned to the logistics function should engage in a variety of activities to account for equipment, supplies, facilities, vehicles, and more used during the event. Some illustrations of wrap up activities by logistics staff are shown below.

Illustrations of logistics wrap-up activities include the following:

- Retrieve all department supplies and equipment from all personnel and event locations (check against computerized inventory)

- Return all internally acquired resources to applicable divisions

- Collect and store all temporarily issued equipment (riot shields and gear, etc.)

- Return all leased equipment to suppliers

- Inspect all facilities used by security personnel

- Return any unused munitions to storage or suppliers, if applicable

- Return any specially modified equipment to its intended use (vehicles, shotguns, etc.)

- Restore all facilities to regular operational status (property room, store rooms, etc.).

Accounting Functions

The main accounting functions that are involved in closing out event security operations include receiving all invoices from suppliers; invoices from other agencies for personnel overtime, supplies, mileage, etc.; and paying any other security-related expenses. The accounting staff will also need to process any internal agency personnel actions (e.g., overtime vouchers, injury reports, compensatory time requests, etc.).

The accounting staff should also prepare a final report showing all expenditures related to security for the event. Itemized details should be attached to the summary.

After-Action Report

An after-action report or event security critique provides the lead agency and event organizers with a final report that documents the nature of the event, what activities occurred during the event, what security efforts were implemented, what went well, what didn't go well, and what lessons were learned. The after-action report should cover, in detail, each specific area of the security plan and operation—including communications, access control, transportation, intelligence, credentialing, logistics, fire/EMS, training, and more.

The purpose of the plan is to (1) document what functions and activities occurred during the event (e.g., spectator problems or incidents); (2) document what security was implemented—and whether it was implemented according to the security operations plan; (3) identify what security actions were done correctly and worked; (4) identify what security actions were implemented incorrectly, the reasons why, and the consequences; and (5) make recommendations for what should be retained and changed for security at future events. Some of the overarching areas that should be emphasized in conducting event security critiques include use of technology (including equipment and information systems), communications (internal and external), training, availability of personnel resources, interaction with partner agencies, and fiscal resources.

There are several varying methodologies for conducting after-action inquiries. Some common examples follow (partner agencies must be included in all evaluations):

- Supervisors complete individual critiques (use standardized questions). If the event continues over more than one day, they complete a report for each day (so they don't forget small details).

- Members of the event evaluation team conduct debriefing interviews with event security supervisors, commanders, and others.

- Focus groups are held with event security commanders and supervisors to discuss the issues.

- Event evaluators spend time in the field during the event to collect their own observations and critiques.

Appendix A

Federal Law Enforcement Representatives Interviewed
and Others (*) Who Assisted in Reviewing the Guideline

Dr. Mary Kay Armour
Instructional Systems Specialist*
U.S. Secret Service

Jeffrey C. Bedford
Supervisory Special Agent*
Federal Bureau of Investigation

Andrew K. Bettencourt
Instructional Systems Specialist*
U.S. Secret Service

Alan Brown, Director of Special Events
U.S. Department of Defense

Basil (Biff) Brown, Associate Director*
U.S. Department of Homeland Security

Craig Caldwell, SAIC, Atlanta
U.S. Secret Service

Russ Collett, ATSAIC, Chicago
U.S. Secret Service

Floyd Dixon, SAIC, Oklahoma City
U.S. Secret Service

Frank Fitzpatrick, Planner/Logistician
U.S. Department of Defense

Tom Kasza, SAIC Chicago
U.S. Secret Service

Jeff Krivak, ATSAIC
U.S. Secret Service

Craig Olson, Unit Chief
Federal Bureau of Investigation

James Perro, ATSAIC
U.S. Secret Service

Keith Prewitt, Assistant Director
U.S. Secret Service

Bruce Townsend, Deputy Assistant Director
U.S. Secret Service

Robert (Bo) Trumbo, ATSAIC*
U.S. Secret Service

Kristen Von Kleinsmid, Supervisory Special Agent*
Federal Bureau of Investigation

Malcolm Wiley, ATSAIC, Atlanta
U.S. Secret Service

Dave Wilkinson, SAIC, Atlanta
U.S. Secret Service

Local Law Enforcement Representatives Interviewed

Captain Chuck Adkins
Charlotte-Mecklenburg (North Carolina) Police Department

Captain Tim Alban
Tulsa County (Oklahoma) Sheriff's Office

Lieutenant Mark Askerlund
Salt Lake City (Utah) Police Department

Lieutenant Rick Aversano
Pasadena (California) Police Department

Major John Ball
Indianapolis (Indiana) Police Department

Lieutenant Karl Barth
Columbus (Ohio) Police Department

Deputy Chief Mike Batista
Denver (Colorado) Police Department

Commander Lynnae Berg
Portland (Oregon) Police Bureau

Chief Ron Burns
Lakewood (Colorado) Police Department

Captain Patrick Carroll
University of California Police Department
Berkeley Campus

Deputy Chief James A. Cervera
Virginia Beach (Virginia) Police Department

Lieutenant Eugene Cummings
Philadelphia Police Department

Assistant Chief Robert Dahlstrom
Austin (Texas) Police Department

Assistant Chief W. K. David
Jacksonville (Florida) Sheriff's Office

Deputy Inspector John K. Donohue
New York City Police Department

Officer Ed Doyle
Cook County (Illinois) Sheriff's Police Department

Superintendent Robert Dunford
Boston Police Department

Major Neil Flood
Monroe County (New York) Sheriff's Office

Lieutenant Don Flower
San Diego County (California) Sheriff's Department

Chief Dan Flynn
Savannah-Chatham (Georgia) Metropolitan Police Department

Deputy Commissioner Patricia Giorgio-Fox
Philadelphia Police Department

Lieutenant Anselmo Gonzales
Los Angeles County Sheriff's Department

Lieutenant Jeff Halstead
Phoenix (Arizona) Police Department

Robert Hardin, Intelligence Commander
Georgia Bureau of Investigation

Chief Victoria Harrison
University of California Police Department
Berkeley Campus

Lieutenant Donald Hawkins
Nashville (Tennessee) Police Department

Lieutenant Aimee Henderson
Prince George's County (Maryland) Police Department

Chief A. L. Kelly
Jacksonville (Florida) Sheriff's Office

Inspector Robert Lucena
New York City Police Department

Director Frank Mackesy
Jacksonville (Florida) Sheriff's Office

Captain Tony Narris
San Diego County (California) Sheriff's Department

Chief Inspector Joseph O'Connor
Philadelphia Police Department

Sergeant Tom Page
Las Vegas Metro Police Department

Captain Eddie Reyes
Alexandria (Virginia) Police Department

Lieutenant Rick Seibler
Jacksonville (Florida) Sheriff's Office

Chief Dwain Senterfitt
Jacksonville (Florida) Sheriff's Office

Commander Rosie Sizer
Portland (Oregon) Police Bureau

Captain Kerry Sweet, Senior Police Attorney
New York City Police Department

Captain Stephen Tacchini
San Francisco Police Department

Assistant Chief Michael Tiffany
New York City Police Department

Inspector Robert Turk
Nassau County (New York) Police Department

Lieutenant Mark Vennemeier
Cincinnati (Ohio) Police Department

Chief Matt Weathersby
Orange County (Florida) Sheriff's Office

Deputy Chief Harry Wedin
New York City Police Department

Private Sector Security Representatives Interviewed

Milton E. Ahlerich, Vice President, Security
National Football League

Richard Avery, Regional President (New England)
Securitas

Tim Christine, Director of Security
NASCAR

William Cunningham, President
Hallcrest Systems, Inc.

Peter Kranske, Security Director
Contemporary Services Corporation

Margaret Levine, Director of Security
Georgia Power Company

Bob Mosley
Communications Specialist AGILE Project
National Institute of Justice

Peter Ohlhausen, President
Ohlhausen Research, Inc.

Tom Seamon, Co-Chair
Private Sector Liaison Committee
International Association of Chiefs of Police

Michael Seddes, Director of Security
New Hampshire International Speedway

John Strauchs, President
Systech Group, Inc.

Regional Special Events Reviewed

Lead Local Agency	Event	Date
Austin (Texas) Police Department	Mardi Gras	February 2004
Charlotte-Mecklenburg Police Department	Coca Cola 600 Speed Street Festival	May 2004
Cincinnati Police Department	Riverfest	September 2004
Columbus (Ohio) Police Department	Red, White and Blue festival	July 4, 2004
Lead Local Agency	**Event**	**Date**
Denver Police Department	Bronco Super Bowl Celebration	January 2004
Indianapolis Police Department	Indiana Black Expo Summer Celebration	July 2004
Jacksonville (Florida) Sheriff's Office	NBA Olympic Warmup Game	July 2004
Las Vegas Metro Police Department	World Championship Boxing (De La Hoya v. Moseley)	September 13 2003,
Los Angeles County Sheriff's Department	Christopher St. Gay and Lesbian Pride Parade	June 2004
Monroe County (New York) Sheriff's Office	PGA Championship	August 2003
Nashville Police Department	Nashville July 4th Celebration	July 4, 2004
Nassau County (New York) Police Department	US Open Golf Tournament	June 2002
Orange County (Florida) Sheriff's Office	NATO Parliamentary Conference	November 7, 2003
Pasadena (California) Police Department	Tournament of Roses Parade/Rose Bowl Game	December 31- January 1, 2004

Lead Local Agency	Event	Date
Philadelphia Police Department	Freedom Day 4th of July Parade	July 4, 2004
Phoenix Police Department	Phoenix July 4th Celebration	July 4, 2004
Portland (Oregon) Police Bureau	Fat Tuesday Celebration	February 2004
Salt Lake City Police Department	Semi-Annual LDS Church Conferences	April and October 2004
San Diego County (California) Sheriff's Department	San Diego County Fair	June-July 2004
San Francisco Police Department	Chinese New Year Parade	February 2004
Tulsa County (Oklahoma) Sheriff's Office	Tulsa State Fair	September-October 2003
Lead Local Agency	Event	Date
University of California Police Department/Berkeley Campus	University of California/ Berkeley vs. UCLA Football Game	October 16, 2004
Virginia Beach (Virginia) Police Department	American Music Festival and Rock and Roll Half Marathon	September 2004

National Events Reviewed

- Academy of Achievement Summit, Chicago, Illinois, June 2004

- Democratic National Convention, Boston, Massachusetts, June 2004

- G-8 Summit, Sea Island, Georgia, June 2004

- Kentucky Derby and Derby Breakfast Events, Louisville, Kentucky, May 2004

- Super Bowl XXXIX, Jacksonville, Florida, February 2005

- Presidential Debate, St. Louis, Missouri, October 2004

- Republican National Convention, New York, New York, July 2004

- Sylvania 300 NASCAR Race, New Hampshire International Speedway, September 2004

Appendix B

Selected Bibliography and Other Resources: Planning and Managing Special Events Security

Alpert, G. and D. Flynn. Community policing and major special events: A case study of Super Bowl XXXIII. Chapter 23 in Alpert & Piquero (eds), 2nd Edition, *Community policing: Contemporary readings,* Waveland, 2000.

Begley, S. "Play ball, but ban the backpacks." *Newsweek,* 138(19), 30-32, 2001.

Berlonghi, A. *The special event risk management manual.* Mansfield, Ohio, Bookmasters Inc., Revised 1994.

Bonner, J. "Looking for faces in the Super Bowl crowd." *Access Control & Security Systems Integration,* 44(3), 1-4, 2001.

Bunis, D., and M. Himmelberg. "No-fly zone over Disney theme parks irks small-plane pilots." [Newspaper Source]. Santa Ana, California, *Orange County Register,* 2003.

Burnside, M. W. "Communication between event and security is a key to success." *Amusement Business,* 114(48), 18, 2002.

Carter, D. *Law enforcement intelligence: A guide for state, local, and tribal law enforcement agencies.* Washington, D.C., Office of Community Oriented Policing Services, U.S. Department of Justice, 2004.

Cole, D. *The incident command system: A 25-year evaluation by California practitioners.* National Fire Academy, Federal Emergency Management Agency, February 2000. www.usfa.fema.gov/downloads/pdf/tr_00dc.pdf.

Chapman, R. et al. *Local law enforcement responds to terrorism.* Washington, D.C., Office of Community Oriented Policing Services, U.S. Department of Justice, 2002.

Cohn, P. "Sports flyover threat provision ends with session." *CQ Weekly,* 60(45), 3086, 2002.

Crowe, Timothy. *Crime prevention through environmental design* (2nd Edition). Woburn, Massachusetts, Butterworth-Heinemann, 2000.

Deckard, L. "Crowd control seminar urges arena managers to stand ground." *Amusement Business,* 112(46), 12, 2000.

Federal Bureau of Investigation. *Special Events Management Planning Handbook.* Washington D.C., FBI, U.S. Department of Justice.

Fussner, J. "Not all fun and games." *Security Management,* 46(8), 84-90, 2002.

Gips, Michael A. "An island of protection." *Security Management,* September 2004, 67-79.

Greene, J. et al. *Safety and security at the Olympic Games in Salt Lake City, Utah.* Washington, D.C., Bureau of Justice Assistance, U.S. Department of Justice, 2002.

Himmelberg, M. "Disney's Anaheim, Calif., theme parks will get permanent security gates" [Newspaper Source]. Santa Ana, California, *Orange County Register*, 2004.

Hinton, E. "Massive security effort in place at Indianapolis 500" [Newspaper Source]. Orlando, Florida, T*he Orlando Sentinel*, 2002.

International Association of Assembly Managers (IAAM). Various publications on best practices for safety and security at arenas, stadiums, and other special events. www.iaam.org.

Lister, S. "Spectators given body searches as part of security operation" [Newspaper Source]. London, *The Times*, 2003.

Markel, P. G. "Getting ready for the big day." *Security Management*, 43(7) 46-50, 1999.

Mitchell, F. "Safe spot? At your Secret Service; Super Bowl fans aren't complaining about checkpoints." [Newspaper Source]. Chicago, Illinois, *Chicago Tribune*, 2002.

Morrison, G. and J. Airey. "Special events safety and security." *FBI Law Enforcement Bulletin*, 71(4) 1-5, 2002.

Murphy, Gerald L. et al. *Protecting your community from terrorism: The strategies for local law enforcement series. Vol. 1: Improving Local-Federal Partnerships.* Washington, D.C., Office of Community Oriented Policing Services, U.S. Department of Justice, 2004.

Nichter, A. D. "Staging a successful performance." *Security Management*, 45(1), 108-112, 2001.

O'Connor, T.J. "Before the show begins." *Security Management*, November 2004, 93-97, 2004.

Painter, K. and N. Tilley, eds. *Surveillance of public space, CCTV, street lighting, and crime prevention.* Crime Prevention Studies, Volume 10, Criminal Justice Press, 1999.

Sherwood, C. W. "Security management for a major event." *FBI Law Enforcement Bulletin*, 67(8), 9-16, 1998

Skipitares, C. "California theme parks tighten security" [Newspaper Source]. San Jose, California, *San Jose Mercury News*, March 27, 2003.

The 9/11 Commission Report. *Final report of the National Commission on Terrorist Attacks upon the United States.* National Commission on Terrorist Attacks Upon the United States. New York, New York, W.W. Norton & Company, Inc., 2004.

Whisenant, W. A. "Using biometrics for sport venue management in a post 9-11 era." *Facilities*, 21(5/6), 134-141, 2003

Wolf, J. "The secret to security." *Successful Meetings*, 52(12), 38-41, 2003.

Appendix C

Security Planning Organization Chart for
Jacksonville, Florida, Sheriff's Office and
Super Bowl XXXIX

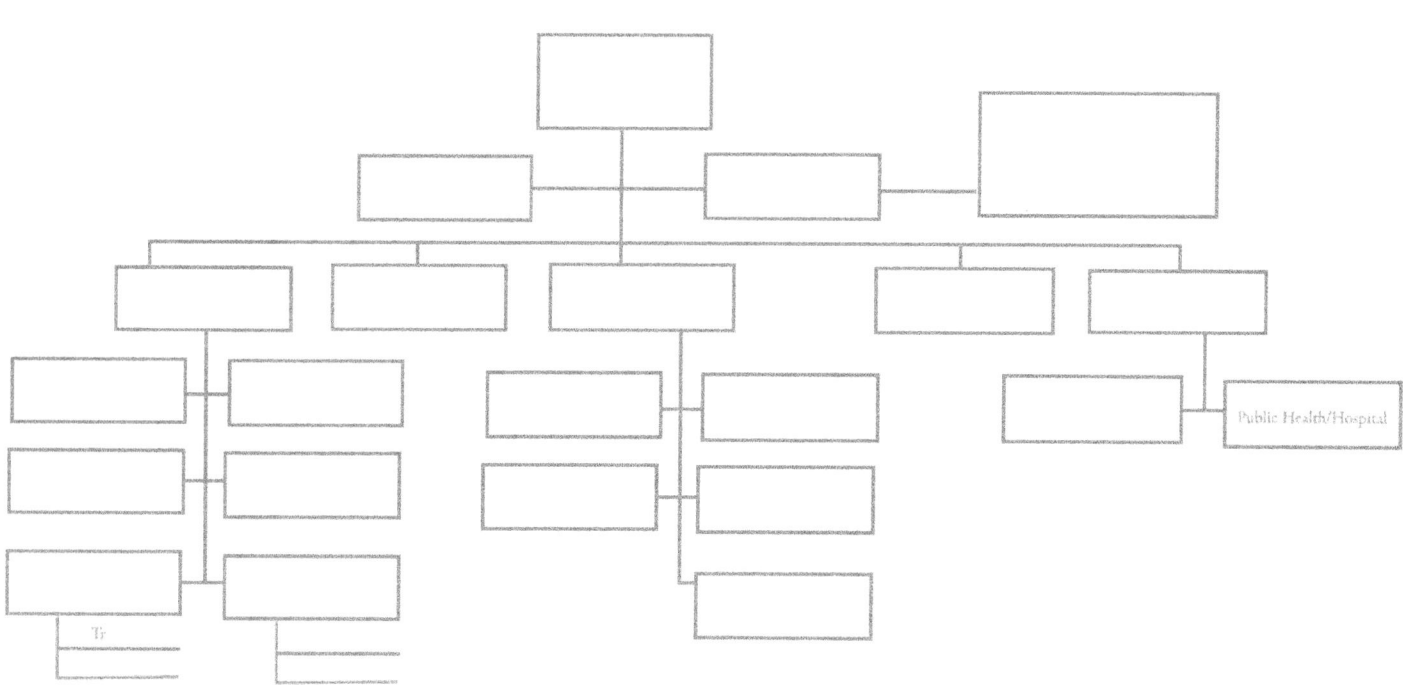

Security Planning Organization Chart for the New York City Police Department and the 2004 Republican National Convention

Organization Structure Used by the New York City Police Department for Planning and Organizing Security for the 2004 Republican National Convention

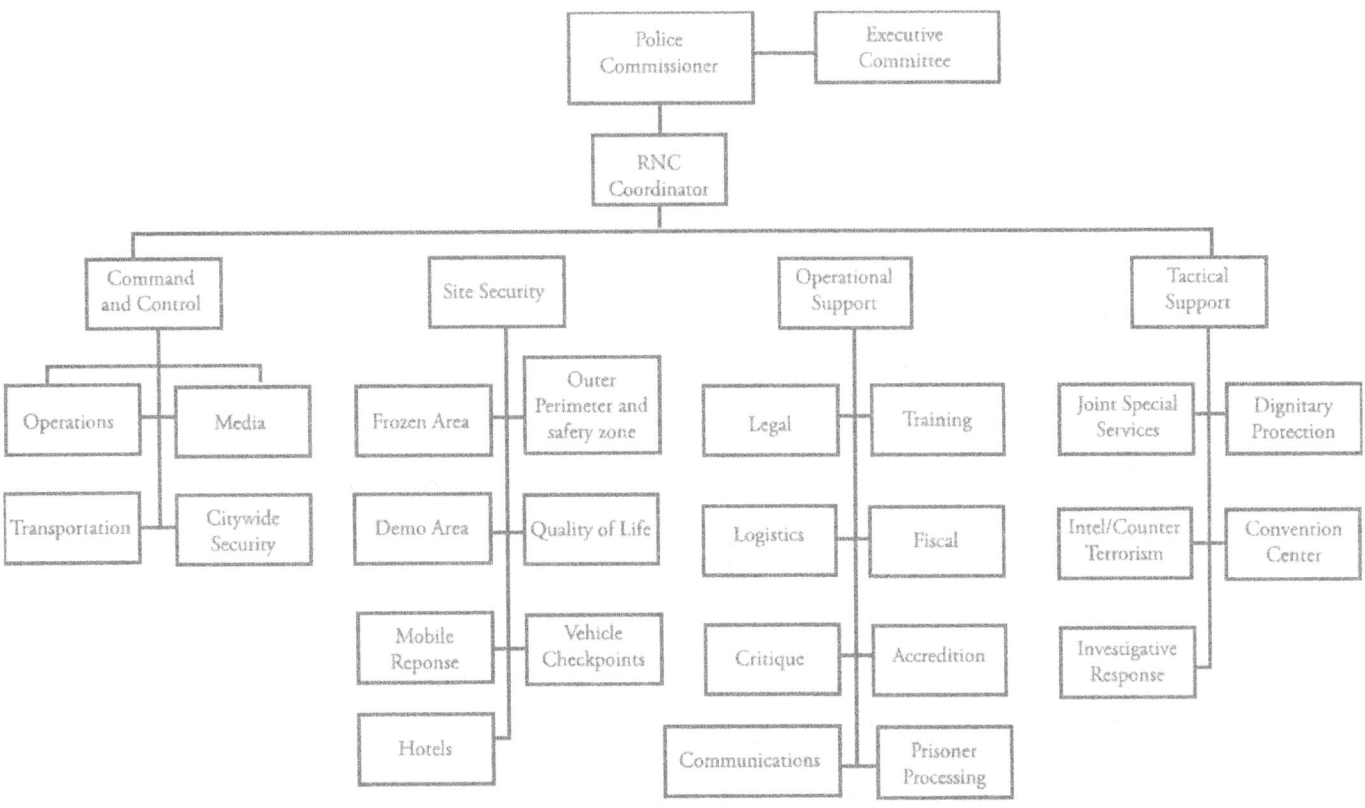

Appendix D

Summary of Key Questions to Ask When Developing the Event Security Plan

1. Determining and Acquiring the Security Workforce

Do we have enough personnel in house?

Who should we partner with for additional security forces?

Who should we partner with for additional authority, skills, equipment, or technology support?

2. Communications and Communication Technology

Do we have a process in place to communicate regularly with all key partners?

Do we have adequate communications technology and equipment?

Do we have adequate communications back-up?

Can we integrate radio communication among many different agencies involved in the event?

Are communications command center facilities adequate in size and scope?

3. Access Control: Screening and Physical Security

Do we have clearly specified perimeters: inner, middle, outer?

Do we have adequate and appropriate security for each perimeter?

Do we have enough technical equipment for effective and efficient screening?

Do we have enough staff for timely screening?

Do we have staff trained and experienced in screening?

Do we have proper screening protocols?

Are screening regulations clearly posted for all participants to read?

4. Transportation/Traffic

Do we have adequate security staffing and assignments for motorcades carrying VIPs?

Do we have adequate motorcade route plans and contingency route plans?

Have all personnel involved in motorcade security been briefed on the plans?

Do we have maps showing anticipated traffic patterns for spectators coming to and leaving the event?

Have we conducted risk assessments for all transportation modes—vehicle traffic, mass transit (buses, subways, trains), marine traffic, and more?

5. Intelligence

Does the lead agency have an effective intelligence capability?

Can we receive support from a state agency with an intelligence capability?

Can we receive support from the local FBI Joint Terrorism Task Force (JTTF)?

Do we have adequate intelligence support to conduct threat and risk assessments?

Do we need to employ intelligence resources in the field during the event?

6. Credentialing

Do we have a plan and process to produce credentials for the special event?

Do we have adequate technology to produce credentials?

Do we have the required personnel contact information in a database to produce credentials?

If we don't have the capacity to produce credentials in-house, what agency can we partner with to help us?

7. Administrative and Logistics Support

Do we have a designated administrative logistics coordinator?

Have we developed a task and timeline to manage the administrative and logisti-cal needs?

Do we have an adequate inventory of needed equipment, supplies, and other items to provide security at the special event?

Which other agencies can we work with to borrow or lease needed equipment, vehicles, and other logistical support items?

Are we prepared to make timely purchases of any equipment or supplies that we need to acquire for the event?

Do we have an adequate budget to support the security needs of the special event?

8. Protecting Critical Infrastructure and Utilities

Have we conducted risk assessments on critical infrastructure and utilities that could impact the special event?

Have we collaborated with infrastructure and utilities managers to develop adequate security plans?

Have we coordinated with sanitation services for event security support?

Have we considered protective measures for cyber systems in event of attack?

9. Fire/EMS/Medical Care

Have we developed adequate plans for fire and EMS services' response if needed at the event?

What numbers and types of personnel are needed at the event?

What types of apparatus, medical vehicles, and equipment are needed at the event?

Have we coordinated adequately with a hospital to handle any casualties?

10. Hazardous Materials/Weapons of Mass Destruction: Detection and Consequence Management

Do we give adequate consideration in our security planning to detecting threats

from explosives and from radiological, chemical, and biological agents and bombs?

Do we have an adequate consequence management plan?

Do we have adequate protocols for handling bomb threats?

Do we have an adequate emergency evacuation plan?

11. Tactical Support and Crisis Management

Do we have local specialized tactical resources (SWAT teams)?

Do the threat and risk levels for the special event require involving the tactical resources?

Have security planners coordinated with the local FBI for crisis management support?

12. Public Information and Media Relations

Have we developed an adequate public information and media relations plan as part of our event security operations plan?

Have we identified the event public information specialist who will coordinate all public and media information?

If the event involves planned demonstrations, have event organizers, government officials, and law enforcement developed a consistent message regarding demonstration activities?

13. Training

Have we conducted a comprehensive training needs assessment to identify all specialized knowledge and skills needed to implement the event security plan?

Have we developed training in key specialized areas for security personnel for this event?

Do we have sufficient training resources in-house or among our partner agencies?

Have we developed the most effective and efficient training methods to reach re-quired personnel prior to the event?

Do we evaluate all training to determine what is effective?

14. Planning for and Managing Demonstrations

Have we received useful intelligence information to advise the security plan on anticipated protest movements at the event?

Do we have adequate support from police legal advisors?

Do we have sufficient numbers of trained mobile field forces to make mass arrests if necessary?

Have we issued rules of engagement to all field forces involved in event security?

Appendix E

Guiding Principles for Major Special Event Security

- Ensure that timely and effective planning, communication, and training are prioritized. Jurisdictions handling special events on a routine basis should consider building events security training into basic and in-service training.

- Understand that overall management of special events is temporary—it involves developing new organizational arrangements, new relationships, and new structures. It is like managing a multi-agency temporary organization. As Professor Jack Green noted in the report on the Salt Lake City Olympics, "The key challenge in this context is to forge new relationships in a time-limited way that can bridge difficult challenges. This may be the key challenge in the entire safety and security operation." (Greene 2002).

- Plan for and manage for the worst-case scenarios.extraordinary crime (and depending on the event, extreme protestors' activities) and possible terrorist attack.but really be prepared to deal with the most ordinary and mundane crimes (pickpockets, thefts from autos, and vandalism) and common civil disruptions (fighting, drunkenness, and disorderly conduct).

- Anticipate unplanned activities and spur of the moment gatherings.for example, on the eve of a major event (Super Bowl, World Series game).

- Secure all perimeters including those in outer areas. In large special events, law enforcement must secure a series of perimeters (inner, middle, and outer). These often involve specific facilities and well-defined territorial venues. However, law enforcement must also be responsible for safety and security in the "theater"—the broader "unbounded" areas of the city or county where other events may occur or VIPs stay in hotels. (Greene, 2002).

- Realize that law enforcement needs to be concerned not only with the safety and security of participants and the event venue, but also the economics of the event. Many events involve commerce, have a budget, and provide income to the local economy.

- Recognize the need for and benefits of leveraging resources and collaborating with other law enforcement agencies; federal agencies; public safety (fire/EMS); other city, county, and state agencies (health, building codes, transportation, parks & recreation); and private security.

- Develop an effective interoperable communications capability if multiple agencies are involved in the field.

- Involve citizens and the business community in planning efforts.

- Ensure that the event continues safely and at the same time respect Constitutional rights including freedom of speech and assembly.

- Ensure that the rest of the jurisdiction receives essential law enforcement services, regardless of the size or importance of the event.

- Evaluate continuously and review operations and practices to update and improve security. Prepare an after-action report after each event.

- Ensure that appropriate federal officials, such as DHS State Homeland Security Advisors, are informed in advance about events with national or international significance to guarantee federal awareness and possible support.